Hosting the Olympic Games

T0386193

Hosting the Olympic Games reveals the true costs involved for the cities that hold these large-scale sporting events. It uncovers the financing of the Games, reviewing existing studies to evaluate the costs and benefits, and draws on case study experiences of the Summer and Winter Games from the past forty years to assess the short- and long-term urban legacies for host cities.

Written in an easily accessible style and format, it provides an in-depth critical analysis into the franchise model of the International Olympic Committee (IOC) and offers an alternative vision for future Games. This book is an important contribution to understanding the consequences for the host cities of Olympic Games.

John Rennie Short is a Professor in the School of Public Policy, University of Maryland, Baltimore County, USA. His research interests include cities, history of cartography, and geopolitics. He has published widely in a range of journals and is the author of 47 books. His work has been translated into Chinese, Czech, Japanese, Korean, and Spanish. His essays have appeared in Associated Press, *Business Insider*, *Citiscope*, *City Metric*, *Market Watch*, *Newsweek*, *PBS NewsHour*, *Quartz*, *Salon*, *Slate*, *Time*, *US News and World Report*, *Washington Post*, and *World Economic Forum*.

Hosting the Olympic Games
The Real Costs for Cities

John Rennie Short

Routledge
Taylor & Francis Group

LONDON AND NEW YORK

First published 2018
by Routledge

2 Park Square, Milton Park, Abingdon, Oxfordshire OX14 4RN
52 Vanderbilt Avenue, New York, NY 10017

Routledge is an imprint of the Taylor & Francis Group, an informa business

First issued in paperback 2020

British Library Cataloguing-in-Publication Data
A catalogue record for this book is available from the British Library

Library of Congress Cataloging-in-Publication Data
Names: Short, John R., author.
Title: Hosting the Olympic Games : the real costs for cities / John Rennie
   Short.
Description: Abingdon, Oxon ; New York, NY : Routledge, 2018. |
   Includes bibliographical references and index.
Identifiers: LCCN 2018005621 | ISBN 9781138549463 (hardback) |
   ISBN 9781351000352 (ebook)
Subjects: LCSH: Olympics—Economic aspects. | Olympic host city
   selection—Economic aspects. | Hosting of sporting events—Economic
   aspects.
Classification: LCC GV721.5 .S49 2018 | DDC 796.48—dc23
LC record available at https://lccn.loc.gov/2018005621

ISBN: 978-1-138-54946-3 (hbk)
ISBN: 978-0-367-67047-4 (pbk)

Typeset in Times New Roman
by Apex CoVantage, LLC

Contents

Tables

Figures

1   Setting the scene

I have watched every single Olympic Games, summer and winter, since 1960. I am not alone. The Games are the most-watched event in human history, an athletic competition that draws a worldwide audience. I write these lines as the world is getting ready to witness the opening ceremonies of the 2018 Winter Games in Pyeongchang, South Korea.

The five Olympics rings now have global brand recognition. The Games have evolved into more than just a platform for sporting prowess and athletic brilliance; they are also a television spectacle, a billion-dollar-plus business, an opportunity for corporate sponsorship, and an arena for national expressions and international tensions. These most global of events are also rooted in particular places. The Games shift. Unlike the Games of ancient Greece, they are held in a new location every four years for both Summer and Winter Games. The urban impact of hosting the Games is the subject of this book.

My focus is on the modern Olympic Games. The term 'modern' implies not only the Games of the here and now compared to those of ancient times, but is also a reminder that their emergence and organization represent an important and defining moment of modernity: themes of nationalism and globalism, cultural and economic globalization, the cult of the body, the sports-athletic complex, the rise of a corporate capitalism, the creation of the mega-event, and the global spectacular all take place in and through the Olympic Games. It is not too much of a stretch to make a claim that the Olympics helped to create the modern world. And the modern world, with its blemishes as well as its wonders, is reflected back to us in the Olympic Games.

There are a number of detailed case studies of the impact of individual Games. (A detailed bibliography is included in *A guide to further reading* at the end of the book). There are also studies that focus on specific issues, such as the transport implications, or on econometric cost-benefit analysis. Often, these analyses roll up diverse global mega-events, such as the World Cup and the Games, into one general discussion. This book is distinctive in that it looks across different host cities of the Olympic Games only, to allow a general assessment of the positive and negative impacts on cites of hosting the Olympic Games.

Costs and benefits: winner and losers

The book aims to answer two basic question: what are the real costs? and who pays and who benefits?

There are two possible answers to the first question. There is the winning-gold argument that sees a net benefit to host cities and their citizens. The Games as positive effect on cites is the loudest and, hence, the strongest argument. It is enunciated by powerful business and political groups wishing to host the Games and by the International Olympic Committee (IOC), which, as it gets bigger and richer, exerts a more-powerful force in shaping the narrative about the Olympic Games. Proponents argue that while there may be some inconveniences and costs, cities should host the Games because the benefits outweigh the costs, because the city is guaranteed a great legacy of sports facilities, improved infrastructure, and more-positive global recognition.

This argument is strengthened because globalization pits cities against each other for inward investment, tourists, and enhanced global image. As globalization flattens and shrinks much, but not all, of the world, even small differences between cities are magnified in the relentless drive to be globally competitive. Any possibility of becoming more recognized is widely sought. Hosting the Games, in this narrative, is a potential game-changer, a once-in-a-lifetime opportunity for a city to attract money and jobs and create a lasting positive legacy.

On the other hand, mounting criticisms of hosting the Games argues that the costs outweigh the benefits.[1] The term *event capture* is used to refer to the way that cities, rather than winning gold by hosting the Games, are, in effect, held captured by the Games.[2]

Event capture

Event capture takes four main forms. First, there is *infrastructure capture,* where the city's infrastructure is constructed and reconstructed around the particular needs of an unusual two-week event. Hence, the emphasis is on venues for short-lived sporting events, airport upgrades, and the easing of routes from the airport into and out of the city. This spending distorts the longer-term infrastructure needs of the city. Long-terms plans have to work around the peculiar needs of the Games. Second, there is *financial capture,* in which public monies are devoted to funding the Games, directly and indirectly. There are associated opportunity costs, as other projects are cancelled or much reduced, and social programs are sacrificed to put on the Games. Third, there is *legal capture,* as new legislation is introduced. Limitations are places on citizens' rights in order to secure the financial profitability and the security of the Games. Fourth, there is *political capture,* as the normal rules of accountability and transparency are displaced and eroded by non-elected organizations, such as the IOC and Olympic Committee Organizing Committees that are given prime roles in the life of the city in the lead-up to and during the Games.

Who gains and who loses?

Costs are unequally shouldered and benefits are unevenly realized. Another question needs to be asked: who gains and who loses when cities host the Games? In subsequent chapters, I will try to identify the winners and losers.

The rest of the book will provide answers to these two big questions: what are the real costs of hosting the Games? and who pays and who benefits? But first, we need to place the contemporary Games in an historical context.

Notes

1 Zimbalist, A. (2016, 2nd ed.) *Circus Maximus: The Economic Gamble Behind Hosting the Olympics and World Cup.* Washington, DC: Brookings Institution Press.
2 Müller, M. (2015) The mega-event syndrome: Why so much goes wrong in mega-event planning and what to do about it. *Journal of the American Planning Association* 81: 6–17.

Müller, M. (2016) How megaevents capture their hosts: Event seizure and the World Cup 2018 in Russia. *Urban Geography* 1–20.

2 The Olympics
Past and present

The modern Olympics make claim to a much longer history, a connection with a major foundation of Western civilization, ancient Greece. But, as we shall see, despite the claims to historical associations, the connection is more tenuous than steady, and more improvisational than a simple updating of the original.

Ancient games

The ancient Greeks honored their heroes after they died with running and wrestling competitions, often close to the burial site. A prehistoric tumulus at Olympia, a remote and secluded site close to the city of Elis and 210 miles southwest from Athens, was, according to legend, the burial place of a famous charioteer Pelops. At the foot of Mt. Kronos, close to two small rivers with groves of olive, pine, and oak trees, Olympia emerged as an early site for athletic competitions.

King Iphitos of Elis, almost 3,000 years ago, believed he could save Greece from plague and civil war by reinvigorating athletic competitions in a more formal and Panhellenic form. He invited all of the Greek states to compete at Olympia. The Greeks only started to number their Games for this one held, in 776 BCE. It was a small affair; there was only one race, won by a local athlete. But from this small start, the Games grew to a major event of the Classical world, held every four years for the next 1,200 years.

The Games at Olympia, the original Olympics, were a religious ceremony honoring the Greek god Zeus. The religious devotion to Zeus and the Panhellenic competition cemented the Greek identity. As athletes travelled to the Games and during the competition, a truce was declared between perennially warring city-states. Weapons were barred from the Games. The Olympia Games were not the only games of ancient Greece: at Delphi, games celebrated Apollo, and in Athens they were held in honor of Athena; Poseidon was honored at Corinth, and Zeus at Nemea.

At Olympia, as in the other games, athletes competed for money and honor, their own personal honor and that of the city-states they represented. The site at Olympia contained a hippodrome, a stadium, a swimming pool (for relaxation as there were no swimming events), and a gymnasium, all spread out around the Temple of Zeus that housed a 13-meter-high statue of Zeus, one of the Seven Wonders of the Ancient World.[1]

The Games were held every four years in August. In the spring of an Olympics year, as the warming weather coaxed a profusion of wild flowers in Olympia, heralds from Elis traveled around the Greek world announcing an Olympics truce. Up to 50,000 spectators gathered for the Games, drawn from near and far. The mainland cities of Athens, Corinth, and Sparta were well represented, as were Greek colonies from around the Mediterranean. The later Games were filled with Romans eager to see and experience the Greek world. All contestants had to be freeborn males of Greek descent. Women, slaves, and foreigners (barbarians to the Greeks) were not allowed to participate. Only unmarried women were allowed to attend the Games. A women's race was held every four years between the main Games, and the winner had her likeness painted on the walls of the Temple of Hera that sat close to the Temple of Zeus.

Figure 2.1 Olympia, Greece: the site of the Olympic Games from 776 BCE to 426 ACE

Source: John Rennie Short

Olympia was dedicated solely to hosting the Olympics. It lay empty most of the rest of the time and since there were no amenities, the thousands of spectators brought their own tents and shelters and camped out in the heat of summer, with little sanitation. (You could probably have smelled as well as heard the crowds.)

The Games were a five-day event. Athletes arrived as much as a month before the formal start in order to train and prepare. On the first day, athletes took a solemn oath to observe the rules. Because months and even years of training could not guarantee results, some athletes would also make an animal sacrifice to ensure victory. The judges also swore to be fair. On the second day, boys competed in boxing, running, and wrestling. The athletic competitions got underway on the morning of the third day, with chariot races. These were the blue-ribbon events, the cost of good horses making them only open to the very rich. The Roman emperor Nero competed in 65 ACE. He bribed the judges in order to secure a victory (so much for the judges' oath). He was declared the winner, despite the awkward fact that he fell off his chariot before the finish line. In the afternoon came the discuss hurlers and javelin throwers.

On the morning of the fourth day, 100 oxen were sacrificed at the Temple of Zeus and the meat was eaten later that evening at a public banquet. In the afternoon, the runners competed. In the 3,800-meter race, run runners would often try to trip their competitors. The main event was a 192-meter dash. Day four also saw wrestling, boxing, and running in armor – a reminder that the Games owed their origin to forms of martial training. On the final day, victors in each event led competitors and trainers in a procession to the Temple of Zeus. The winners were crowned with a wreath of wild olive. Those able to drum up financial support had statues of themselves placed in the grounds. There were no prizes for those coming in second or third. The afternoon and evening was devoted to celebrations, feasting, drinking, and the singing of hymns of victory as well as the drowning of sorrows of defeat.[2]

Over time, the link between the Games and the worship of Zeus loosened; Alexander the Great built statues of himself at Olympia, making it less a site for religious devotion and more a setting for the cult of personality. The first Roman emperor, Augustus, had one of the temples converted into a shrine to himself. The temples were plundered and their walls pulled down for defensive walls elsewhere. Finally, in ACE 393, the Christian emperor Theodosius, appalled at the pagan nature of the ceremonies, abolished the Games entirely and had all the statues destroyed. The site at Olympia, which had lasted for roughly 1,200 years and hosted 293 consecutive games, was subsequently ravaged by thieves and destroyed by earthquakes, and sank into oblivion.

While the modern Games make a nod to the ancient Games, we should be wary of seeing a straightforward adoption of an ancient tradition. Not only are there the obvious differences – such as the creation of the Winter Games, that had no ancient parallel – but the spirit and conduct of the ancient Games are situated in a very different cultural context from the modern world. The ancient Games were intimately bound up in a profound religious devotion and a Panhellenic celebration that reaffirmed the connection between Greeks and their gods. The Games were a platform for Greek identity.

In the ancient Games, flute music accompanied boxing matches, and long jumpers had to carry weights. And there is a more obvious difference. All the athletes, as well as the trainers, were completely naked: the Greek word for naked is *gymnos*, the source of our word gymnasium. To protect themselves, the athletes rubbed their body with olive oil and smeared on sand.[3]

An invented tradition

The modern Games are not a straightforward modern adoption of an ancient tradition that included such things not seen today: chariot races, naked athletes, animal sacrifices, devotions to Zeus, or flute-accompanied long jumpers and boxers. The modern Olympics are an invented tradition that built on an idealized picture rather than on the actual practice of the ancient Games.[4]

Baron Pierre de Coubertin (1863–1937) first raised the idea of a modern Games. It was not a simple resuscitation but a re-creation in a specific context of growing and intense national competition. The Games were not devised to replace nationalism, but to channel it. Coubertin, the initiator of the modern Games, came from a wealthy French family, and his early interest in sport was situated in a particular class and gendered space. He saw the 1870 French defeat in the Franco-Prussian War as a bitter blow to French self-esteem. The defeat, he believed, was in large part due to the poor physical condition of the French troops, especially compared to the better trained, fitter German troops. His reorganization of French sport was an attempt to rebuild the physical fiber of young Frenchmen. He drew upon the sports tradition of English public schools as one of his models for youthful, male athleticism.

His national concerns widened to the promotion of sport as a forum for peaceful internationalism. After reorganizing a number of French national sports associations, he established the *Union des Societies Francaises de Sports Athletiques*, and in 1892 he revived the notion of the Olympic Games as a forum for international athletic competition. At the end of the 19th century, there were few international sporting organizations or events. Sports were organized along local and national lines. His proposal was part of a growing internationalism.

In the period from around 1870 to 1914, there was rivalry between European powers and the United States for overseas markets and global dominance. The economic and political rivalry reached its peak with the European partition of Africa and the US annexation of the Philippines, Puerto Rico, and Cuba. The major powers were colliding in global space. However, there was also cooperation between countries, as their increasing interaction also promoted shared projects of political and spatial management. Economic integration was an important force. It was a time of low tariffs, an international labor market, and relatively free capital mobility. There was a wave of globalization as the space–time continuum collapsed with the railways, the telegraph, and internationally organized postal unions.

The period is studded with international meetings, conferences, conversations, and conventions that laid down international standards and arrangements. At the Congress of Bern in 1874, 22 countries signed the International Postal Convention. That event set the stage for regular and cheap internal post. The International Workingmen's Association (the first from 1864–1876, the second from 1889–1919) was formed to provide international solidarity of the fledgling workers' movements. The Hague Conventions of 1899 and 1907 codified international rules of war. And the Federation of International Football Associations (FIFA) was formed in Zurich in 1904 to organize the increasingly global sport of soccer. The resurgence of the Games was part of this wider and broader trend of internationalism. Coubertin believed that reviving the ancient Games would counter the worst excesses of nationalism and provide a peaceful forum for international competition.

Coubertin was a product of his time and class. He, and the Games he promoted, embodied elite male attitudes toward class, race, and gender. The ancient Games were professional. The athletes devoted themselves full-time, trained for months and even years leading up the Games, and followed challenging training regimens. They competed for honor and money. The amateurism of the modern Games was not an echo of the ancient world but an explicitly and self-conscious class device to keep out the lower classes. Only the wealthy and privileged could devote themselves to sports without the need for recompense.

The gendered and class and nature of the modern Games is brought into sharper focus by a recognition of the alternatives of the time.

After Alice Millait, a French rower, wrote to the IOC asking to include women athletes in the 1920 Antwerp Olympics and was snubbed, she and others organized the 1921 International Women's Games in Monte Carlo.

Athletes from Britain, France, Italy, Norway, and Sweden attended. The next year, 1922, some 20,000 spectators watched 77 female athletes from five countries compete in the first Women's' Olympic Games in Paris. The IOC did not sanction these events. Subsequent Games were held in Gothenburg in 1926, Prague in 1930, and London in 1934. These Games showed that women could compete in athletics and gymnastics. The official IOC Games had first allowed women to compete in 1900 but restricted their participation to a narrow range of sports. For the IOC 1928 Games, the IOC lifted many of the restrictions, prompted by these insurgent Women's Games, and 290 women from 25 countries competed. In 1936, the French government withdrew its subsidy and the Women's Games collapsed, but they had forced the IOC to consider and approve the participation of female athletes.

The Socialist Workers' Sport International created their own games to promote friendship, solidarity, and peace. The first Workers Olympiad was held in Prague in 1920. The first Worker's Winter Olympiad was held in Germany in 1925. These games were more international than the Olympic Games, because in 1920 and 1924 the IOC did not allow for the participation of the athletes from countries defeated in the First World War. In the Workers' Olympiad, all athletes competed under the red flag of the International Workers' Movement, rather than national flags. The motto of the 1925 Workers' Olympiad in Frankfurt was "No More War." Participation was open to all. More than 100,000 athletes from 26 countries competed in the 1931 Worker's Olympiad in Vienna. The Ernst-Happel Stadium, built in 1929–1931 to house these games, is still the largest outside sporting venue in Austria and hosted the final of the 2008 UEFA Euro soccer tournament. Some 250,000 people came to watch the Workers' Olympiad, almost double the number that went to see the 1932 Summer Olympics in Los Angeles. There were one unofficial and six official Workers' Games. The last scheduled Games of the workers' movement, set for Helsinki in 1943, was cancelled due to World War II.

The Workers' Games, which provided such stiff competition to the Olympic Games for two decades, spluttered and died during World War II. It was the Games of Coubertin – with its class, race and gender biases – that became the undisputed organization for the internationalization of athletics. It is interesting to think of an alternative history if the Workers' Games rather than the Olympic Games had become the more dominant force. The flawed history of international athletics under the Olympics movement – and especially its class, gender, and racial biases; its sham amateurism; and appalling accommodation to Nazism – may have been different and perhaps less dispiriting.

Figure 2.2 The stadium in Athens, Greece, built for the 1896 Games, the first of the modern era. It was used for archery in the 2004 Athens Games

Source: John Rennie Short

Problems along the way

The evolution of the Olympic Games was not a straight-line story of a grow-ing gargantuan success. The growth of the Games was accompanied by problems. Boycotts plagued the Games for a period, while security remains a major and growing concern.

Boycotts

Boycotts used to be a regular feature. Spain and the USSR boycotted the 1936 Games in Berlin. Most other participants should have followed their lead. In 1956, there were three separate boycotts: in 1956, Egypt, Iraq, and Lebanon protested against the Anglo-French-Israeli invasion of Egypt; also in 1956, Cambodia, Netherlands, Spain, and Switzerland protested against the Soviet invasion of Hungary; and in 1976, the People's Republic of China (PRC) pro-tested because the Republic of China (ROC, Taiwan) was allowed to compete. And then there was the decade of boycotts. In 1976, 34 countries boycotted the Montreal Games because of continuing sporting links to the apartheid regime of South Africa. Later, the USA and 65 other countries pulled out of the 1980 Moscow Games to protest the Soviet invasion of Afghanistan. To reciprocate, 18 countries in the Soviet bloc boycotted the 1984 LA Games.

And then the boycotts stopped. The PRC and ROC sorted out their differ-ences, in this sphere at least. The apartheid regime of South Africa fell, as did the Soviet bloc, taking away the perennial East-West fracture in in the global polity. In the past four decades, the Games emerged as a truly global event with participation by most countries and no threat of boycotts.

Security

Just as boycotts seemed to be thing of the past, security became a rising concern. The Olympic Games were strangers to security issues for decades. Munich in 1972 marked a turning point. The 1972 Games were presented as the friendly games. West Germany was eager to join the community of nations, and hosting the Games was a way to wash away some of the sins of World War II, Hitler, and the Holocaust. The atmosphere was more festival like than security conscious. Eight terrorists associated with the Palestinian Black September group entered the athletes' compound and took hostages from the Israeli team. Eleven hostages were killed, five of the terrorists were shot dead by police, and the remaining three were released a month later by the West German government in return for a hijacked Lufthansa jet.

The Games went on. As the IOC embarked on an ambitious plan to glo-balize and commercialize, Munich was discussed, if at all, not as a security failure that needed fixing, but as an unforeseen tragedy. Even the bombing at the 1996 Atlanta Games did not change the narrative. The security issue was swept under the carpet because it threatened to undermine the Games. The IOC offload the cost and organization of the Game to local organizing committees and host cities. They invariably talk up the benefits and downplay the costs. They need to assuage the potential fears of host cities. It is difficult to sell the idea of hosting an event that attracts terrorists and nutjobs, and can only be secured with massive investment in security, policy, and surveillance. For too long, there was a conscious institutional amnesia. Munich devalued the Olympics brand and, hence, had to be forgotten. It was only in 2016 that the IOC officially recognized the horrific event.

Things changed with 9/11. The very success of the Games and their penetration of global media markets make them the juiciest targets for terrorist seeking the oxygen of publicity. The response to the terrorist threat at the Olympics was an increase in security. The Athens Games rang up huge debts, but as the first Summer Games after 9/11, some of the spiraling cost was due to the new need for increased security in the wake of the Twin Towers crashing to the ground. Security costs continue to spiral ever upward, and even when the Games are finished, host cities are left with a legacy of securitized and heavily policed urban public spaces. Hosting the Games now means a permanent security apparatus legacy for citizens.

As the Games grew, they became an ideal platform for acts of terrorism, rogue regimes seeking to make a media splash, or nihilistic bombers desperate for coverage of their savagery. And this is where the security threat and boycotts may overlap, as national governments may need to assess the security risks of exposing athletes to heightened threats. It is unlikely that we are entering a round of boycotts similar to the 1976–1984 era, but the recent example of France's threatened boycott of the Winter 2028 Games may represent a new headache for the IOC.

The Games used to be a sporting event – now they are the worlds' largest security risk. This fact need not lead to the abandonment of the Games, but we do need a serious conversation about the threats and the costs of those Games.

The basic organization of the Games

The modern Olympic Games evolved since the first one held in Athens in 1896. Over the years, new traditions were grafted on – such as the construction of an Olympic Village, the torch relay, the athletes entering the area at the end of the competition – as the Games adapted, changed, and turn innovations into traditions. The Olympic Flame was first introduced in Amsterdam in 1928. The torch relay, involving the transfer of a 'sacred' flame from

Olympia to the host site, was invented for the 1936 Berlin Games and was used to solidify Nazi support and German identity in Central and Eastern Europe. Both are now part of the accepted tradition of the modern Games. The invention of tradition involves the embedding of the provisional and new to become the standard and the established.

The Games are best understood as an organization concerned with moving into the future by repeating the successes of the past while accommodating the pressures of the present. There were and remain many pressures to change, including getting rid of the sham amateurism and hosting more events for women, while adding new sports and events. The Olympics transform over the years. However, there are two basic unchanging characteristics at the heart of the Olympics movement that continue to have profound influence.

The first is the basic organizational structure. The International Olympic Committee (IOC) awards the Games to particular sites and captures most of the revenue. Coubertin established the IOC in 1894 as the governing body of the Olympics movement. In order to protect it from the influence of powerful national governments, he established it as an international organization headquartered in Switzerland. This made it free from national interference and allowed it to hide from scrutiny and avoid transparency. It currently consists of 100 members. It is neither democratic nor transparent. Members include the titled and connected, rather than the disciplined and meritorious. European royalty entranced Coubertin and the early IOC was stuffed with titled members. The commitment to royalty and the rich persists. Current members include Princess Nora of Luxembourg, Prince Albert of Monaco, Princess Anne of the United Kingdom, the Grand Duke of Luxembourg, Prince Frederick of Denmark, Prince Feisal of Jordan, Baron Beckers-Vieujant of Belgium. Juan Antonio Samaranch, a Franco apparatchik who was president of the IOC from 1980 to 2001, demanded treatment similar to ambassadors of nation-states and requested that he be referred to as His Excellency. The King of Spain made him the Marquis of Samaranch in 1991. And in line with the principle of royal succession, his son Juan Antonio Samaranch Salisachs was made an IOC member in 2001. Jacques Rogge, president of the IOC from 2001 to 2013, was made Count Rogge by the King of Belgium in 2002. In status-obsessed IOC, even royal titles from the King of Belgium count for something. We are light years away from the Workers' Games.

After the scandal of Salt Lake City, when IOC members were charged with accepting bribes in return for votes, the IOC membership was changed. Currently, there are 70 members elected by existing members, with the rest drawn from former athletes, National Organizing Olympic Committees, and international sport federations.

While IOC membership has widened, due in part to the globalization of the Games, and members now come from all over the world, they share a similar position of well-compensated volunteers. They are members of an organization handling billions of dollars, with little oversight, regulation, or direct scrutiny. Membership in the IOC often means IOC business intermingles with private business interest. The IOC remains what is was set up to be, an elite group cushioned from popular accountability. It is an undemocratic organization responsible to no one but itself, set up in Switzerland, just like FIFA, to make it impervious to international scrutiny. A product of an elitist class bias, it is insulated from the rough and tumble of democratic discourse or popular accountability. It is a self-serving institution that wraps itself around the flag of a benign Olympics movement.[5]

There is an Executive Board, consisting of the president, four vice-presidents, and 10 other members elected in a secret ballot. Since the reforms of 1999, the Executive Board is now the power center of the IOC, responsible for finances and the bidding process.

The IOC is a self-policing nongovernment organization, a law unto itself without international regulation or oversight. Press scrutiny and corporate concern has increased over the years and especially since a series of scandals over the past 30 years. But what makes the IOC so powerful is its uncontested and monopoly power over the most-watched events in human history.[6]

The second abiding characteristic is that the modern Games, unlike the ancient Games, moves from site to site. From the beginning, it was assumed that the Games would move around, in order to avoid one country dominating the event and to spread the event. In order to build up international support, the Games were to be a mobile event, with different countries able to host the event. In 1894, the IOC decided to host the 1896 Games in Athens and the next one in 1900 in Paris.

There were early campaigns to host the Games permanently in Greece. At the 1896 Games, the King of Greece made a passionate appeal to permanently host the Games in his country. Later, the Greek Parliament even passed a bill that proposed Greece as the permanent site and lobbied to host the games in 1898, 1910, and 1914. They did host an unofficial Games in 1906.

But Coubertin was against a permanent home. Political instability in Greece and military conflict in the Balkans in the early years of the modern Games made it easy to nix the idea of a permanent home in Greece. But there were strategic reasons: a permanent home reduced the power of the IOC, and gave it to the permanent hosts. Moving the Games also drummed up support for the fledgling event by holding out to a range of countries the possibility of hosting the Games. Later, when the Game became more popular, this mobility allowed the IOC to use inter-city competition to their advantage.

In the very early years, however, the site of the Games was not entirely in the grasp of Coubertin or the IOC. He wanted and got the 1900 Games in Paris. But the 1904 Games were initially scheduled for Chicago before they were moved to St. Louis, and Coubertin favored Rome for the 1908 Games but they went to London. Berlin made a strong case for the 1912 Games, but Coubertin favored Stockholm and promised the Germans the 1916 Games. With the 1912 Stockholm Games, the system of awarding the Games was solidified. Henceforth, the IOC would award the Games to a different city every four years. The rotation allowed the IOC to keep control by awarding the Games. The IOC controlled the revenue, while the costs, as we shall see in the next chapter, were borne by the national committees and the host cities.

Notes

1 Swaddling, J. (2015, 3rd ed.) *The Ancient Olympic Games*. London: British Museum Press and University of Texas Press.
2 Woff, R. (1999) *The Ancient Greek Olympics*. New York: Oxford University Press.
3 Perottet, T. (2004) *The Naked Olympics: The True Story of the Ancient Games*. New York: Random.
4 Guttman, A. (2002, 2nd ed.) *The Olympics: A History of The Modern Games*. Urbana and Chicago: University of Illinois Press.
5 Boykoff, J. (2016) *Power Games: A Political History of the Olympics*. London and New York: Verso.
6 Goldblatt, D. (2016) *The Games: A Global History of the Olympics*. New York and London: W. W. Norton.

3   Financing the Games

There is a scene in the movie *All The President's Men* about the Watergate scandal, where the secretive inside source tells the young journalists 'follow the money' as a guiding principle to reveal answers. So, let us take that advice and follow the money of the Olympic Games.

Franchising the Games

The most appropriate model to understand the financing of the Olympic Games is the franchise model. The IOC holds the franchise for the Olympic Games, which it then rents out to host cities. But it is a franchise with a twist, as the IOC retains control over the Games and pockets much of the revenues, but is neither responsible for hosting or paying for the Games nor at risk if any losses occur. In short: a sweet deal for the IOC.

While the IOC has the monopoly power to award the Games, they need cities to host the Games. The emphasis of the early modern Game was, and still is, on cities rather than on nation-states, in order to avoid the narrow nationalism associated with nation-states hosting the Games. It was the Athens and Paris Games, not the Greek or French Games. This city designation lasts to this day. It was the Beijing and Rio Games, not the Chinese or Brazilian Games. But while cities may give their names to the Games, they are rarely capable, on their own, of financing the Games. They need extra funding that comes from a variety of sources, including the private sector, National Olympic Committees (NOCs), and national, regional, and city governments. Many national governments are often directly involved in underwriting the Games.

Revenues

Hosting the Games in the early years was a very risky proposition. They had barely managed to achieve European, never mind global, recognition. Athletic venues needed financing but there was no guarantee that people would come. Not a case of "build it and they will come." More like, "build it and maybe they might come." And so, the early Olympics were very small-scale events by necessity, with little new building. With no dedicated revenue streams, the financing of the Olympic Games was a haphazard affair. The Greek royal family and a rich Greek businessman largely funded the 1896 Athens Games, with the Greek government stepping in to provide loans for the construction of a velodrome and shooting range.

Because the early Games funding was so precarious, they often piggy-backed on the then-more-popular World's Fairs. The early Games were an upstart compared to the more established World's Fairs. The 1900 and 1904 Games were basically a side event to the World's Fairs held in Paris and St Louis, respectively. The 1908 Games in London, an afterthought to the Franco-British Imperial Exhibition held at Earl's Court, were funded by entrepreneur Imre Kiralfy, who built the stadium in return for three-quarters of gate ticket sales. The 1912 Games in Stockholm purposely coincided with a national song competition, to ensure larger crowds.

By the 1920 Games, awarded to Antwerp in 1913 ahead of Amsterdam, Budapest, and Rome, a new pattern had emerged. The Games were pro-moted by the city's financial and political elite, who benefited greatly from the event. In a pattern to be repeated again and again, private interests did well, while the costs were borne by the public. Antwerp was the first city to see the Games as a great opportunity to privatize the benefits, while making the public responsible for the costs. A private elite athletic club used the Games to upgrade their facilities and an already rich family, who owned land around the Olympic stadium, got windfall gains, while the NOC, the national government, and, ultimately, Belgian taxpayers picked up the defi-cits. As two historians noted,

> the Olympic Games of Antwerp are an excellent example of how a wealthy elite can exploit an Olympics event for its own economic advantage and prestige . . . a small group of prominent citizens of large fortune had succeeded in using the Games for their own financial advantage and social prestige.[1]

With the first bid of the City of Los Angeles, the bidding to host the Games became more separated from national political considerations and included the hopes and aspirations of particular city-regions. Los Angeles made a bid for the Games as early as 1923, initiated by an IOC member from Los Ange-les, William May Garland. He was chairman of the local Community Devel-opment Association and worked closely with the city's business and political elite, especially Harry Chandler, owner of the *Los Angeles Times*. Garland was also president of the Chamber of Commerce. The impetus for the Games came from local boosters, business leaders, and real estate interests, a constellation of interests often referred to as the "urban growth machine."[2] The 1932 Games explicitly were employed to boost the city's image, economy, and business fortunes. Proposed at the time of boom, they were also used to stimulate the local economy as an economic recession turned into the Great Depression. The real estate and building interests lobbied for an Olympic Village. Initiated as a building contract, the concept became part of the invented tradition of the modern Olympics, and now all Games consider an Olympic Village part of the assumed infrastructural investment.

The Games require huge public subsidies, often from national governments. This was, and still is, easier in authoritarian or totalitarian systems. The 1936 Games were funded in large part by the German government as part of an agenda to promote the Nazi regime and its ideology. The 1980 Games in Moscow, the 2008 Games in Beijing, and the 2014 Winter Games in Sochi received direct and indirect finding from their respective national governments. In more-democratic countries, the public subsidies are often hidden in a maze of accounting, justified with reference to debatable cost-benefits analysis, or are simply ignored. As the subsidies became larger, however, the criticisms increase. More of this later.

Figure 3.1 The main stadium for the 1976 Montreal Games. The huge direct-cost overruns caused a change in the financing model and a shift from only new building on green fields sites to include the refurbishment of existing facilities

Source: John Rennie Short

A new model

Up until the 1980s, the financing of the Games relied on traditional sources, including public subsidies, revenue from the sale of tickets, memorial coins and stamps, and official mascots. There was a limit to how much these streams could generate. And as the Games became more expensive and costs rose, the fiscal gap widened. The 1960 Rome Olympics cost $50 million, the Munich Games of 1972 cost $850 million, but the Montreal Games reached an astounding $1.5 billion. The Montreal Games were a pivotal movement because they revealed the chasm between limited revenues and ambitious aspirations. Broadcasting rights only generated $35 million in revenue as costs soared with an ambitious and costly new stadium and complex built on a green field side. The result: a huge deficit, estimated at around $1.2 billion. The taxpayers of Montreal and the Province of Quebec were on the hook to make up the difference. A tobacco tax that lasted into the 21st century, 2006 to be precise, eventually paid off the debt.

After the financial debacle of the 1976 Montreal Games, few cities wanted to host the Games. The costs, both financial and political, were too prohibitive. As the only candidate for the 1984 Games – the 1980 Games had already been awarded to Moscow – Los Angeles had the power to introduce a new form of financing, with emphasis on minimizing direct costs and maximizing broadcasting rights and corporate sponsorship. A Los Angeles Olympic Organizing Committee (LAOOC) was established to ensure that taxpayers would not have to meet the costs. The LAOOC was a private organization separate from the City of Los Angeles. In order to cut costs, the LAOCC used existing stadium and facilities rather than building new and expensive facilities, increased broadcasting revenue, and developed corporate sponsorship.

The 1984 Games used the stadium built for the 1932 Games, the Memorial Coliseum, and utilized existing athletic facilities from around the metro region, including Dodgers Stadium, the Rose Bowl, and the Santa Anita racetrack. The existing dormitories of local universities were used to house athletes. The clever use of existing facilities substantially reduced costs. This strategy was employed in later Games to rein in costs, even such extravagant Games as Beijing 2008.

Another change was the extraction of more revenues from broadcasting rights. The LAOOC negotiated a $225 million deal with ABC for 180 hours of television coverage, an amount that was triple what was paid for the 1980 Games. Los Angeles inaugurated the era of large and lucrative broadcasting deals.

Business sponsorship was always an integral part of the modern movement. The very first Games in Athens were dependent on the largesse of a

Greek businessman. In 1912, 10 Swedish companies were given sole rights to all the photographic images of the Games. The 1960 Rome Olympics had 46 private sponsors. Montreal 1976 had 742 business sponsors, and even Moscow 1980 had 200 product endorsements. The 1984 Los Angeles Games shifted the sponsorship model from a large number of small businesses to a smaller number of larger sponsors with global aspirations. Prior to 1984, business sponsors provided only around 10 percent of total revenues. The LAOOC designated 34 corporate sponsors, including Coca-Cola, Mars, and Anheuser Busch, who each paid between $4 million and $15 million for the exclusive right to market their products with the Olympic logo. Twenty percent of the total revenues of $1,124 million of the 1984 Olympics, more than $200 million, came from these corporate sponsors. Since then, corporate sponsorship has increased in both an absolute and relative sense. Now, roughly 40 percent of all IOC revenues come from corporate sponsorship.

Los Angeles 1984 marked a change in the financing of the Games. The LA model minimized expenditure and maximized revenues through selling broadcasting rights and attracting major corporate sponsorship. The LA

Figure 3.2 Opening ceremonies of the 1984 LA Games that marked a new form of financing and greater use of existing facilities. The main stadium, the Los Angeles Memorial Coliseum, was first built to host the 1932 Games

Source: https://upload.wikimedia.org/wikipedia/commons/f/f2/Olympic_Torch_Tower_of_the_Los_Angeles_Coliseum.jpg

Games mark the beginnings of the close connection between the IOC and major corporate sponsors. The LA Games were the only Summer Games to end up with a surplus.

Financing the IOC

The IOC quickly adopted the revenue model developed by the LAOOC and now relies on broadcasting and corporate sponsorship as their main revenue sources. More than 90 percent of IOC revenue comes from the combination of corporate sponsorship and broadcasting rights.

Corporate sponsorship is organized in a program first introduced in 1985, The Olympic Program (TOP). Under TOP, corporate sponsors are given exclusive global marketing rights to use the Olympic logo in their advertising and promotion, in exchange for financial support and goods and services. The deal runs for four years. In the period 2013 to 2016, the 10 TOP partners were Coca-Cola, Atos, Dow, General Electric, McDonalds, Omega, Panasonic, Proctor and Gamble, Samsung, and Visa. Bridgestone and Toyota became TOP partners in 2017.

The corporatization of the Games is explicit in this excerpt from an official Olympics website:

> As an event that commands the focus of the media and the attention of the entire world for two weeks every other year, the Olympic Games are the most effective international corporate marketing platform in the world, reaching billions of people in over 200 countries and territories throughout the world.[3]

Selected corporations now have a close and symbiotic relationship with the IOC. The Games rely on these corporate sponsors, who in turn use the Games as an advertising platform for global economic penetration.

The TOP program raked in $279 million in 1993–96 (the IOC publishes its financial figures as quadrennials), and that figure increased to $950 million by 2009–2012. Over the period 2001 to 2012, the IOC received $2.47 billion from corporate sponsors under TOP.

While not given any formal voting rights in the IOC, the corporate sponsors wield enormous power. They play a significant role in the siting, timing, and organization of the Games. Corporate sponsors prefer big, accessible markets and especially like the Games to be in large emerging markets. Brazil and China fit the bill, with China a perennial favorite because of the access to a huge domestic market with a new middle class eager to spend and consume. The IOC reluctantly awarded the 2000 Games to Sydney; the corporate favorite of Beijing had to be abandoned in the wake of deaths in

Tiananmen Square. Although Sydney was considered a successful Games for the spectators and athletes, it was not so much for the corporate sponsors. Sydney only gave access to a national population of 19.1 million, and the television coverage was not readily accessible in real time for much of the audience in Europe and North America.

The timing of the Games was also changed to suit corporate marketing campaigns. The Summer and Winter Olympics were held in the same year until 1992, when the Lillehammer Winter Games were held in 1994, just two years after the Winter Games in Albertville in order to have a regular two-year spacing between the Summer and Winter Games. Corporate sponsors found it easier to finance their marketing campaigns in a rolling two-year period.

The corporate sponsors are heavily invested in the Olympic brand and, hence, are very sensitive to any devaluation of the brand, such as occurred with the corruption scandal associated with the bid of Salt Lake City for the 2002 Winter Games. It was the corporate sponsors that forced the IOC to clean up the bid process. The corporate sponsors were worried that they could be associated with a tainted product. Sponsors are concerned with anything that devalues the image of the Games, since this undercuts their marketing campaigns and erodes their corporate image. The IOC is largely immune from general public opinion, insulated from public scrutiny and oversight, but not from the opinion and funding of the corporate sponsors. Corporate sponsors wield effective pressure on the IOC.

The Games are now the most watched televised event in the world. The Rome Olympics of 1960 was broadcast to only 21 countries and territories. Forty years later, the Sydney Games were broadcast to more than 220 countries and territories. It is a similar story for the Winter Olympics. Only 27 countries and territories saw the 1960 Olympics Game in Squaw Valley, but more than 220 could access Sochi in 2014. The audiences are vast and the Games now have global coverage and worldwide saturation. More than 2 billion people watch the Winter Olympics and close to 3.5 billion see the Summer Games.

The IOC owns all the lucrative broadcasting rights for the Games that now constitute the single biggest revenue source. For 1997–2000, these broadcasting fees totaled $1.8 billion and by 2009–2012 they had increased to $3.85 billion. The IOC generates huge sums of money from the sale of broadcasting rights. For the period 2001 to 2012, the IOC received a total of $8.65 billion from the sale of broadcast rights. The rights bundle Summer and Winter Games together in order to ensure television coverage of the less-popular Winter Games. The IOC signs deals with televisions companies representing national markets, including Australia, Canada, and China, as well as regional groupings, such as Europe. Major television companies bid for national exclusive rights. In 2011, NBC paid the IOC $4.38 billion for the exclusive right to broadcast the Games in the USA from 2012 to 2020. In 2014, a new contract amounting to $7.75 billion extended the rights to 2032.

With so much invested, it is often difficult for media companies with massive financial interests to show the Games, the IOC, or the Olympics movement in a very critical light. The reverse: with so much invested, they tend to focus on feel-good stories that enhance the Games, which in turn valorizes the IOC. There is a symbiotic relationship between the IOC and their media partners.

The broadcasters get access to all the events and stream hours of sports to a worldwide audience. It is wildly successful and sometimes great television, with competitive effort and skill and grace and beauty combining with compelling stories of victory and defeat, loss and redemption. Compacted into two weeks, it is a great time to watch sports television.

The major television companies also exercise leverage in the staging of the Games. The US television company NBC, which pays the largest amount for the US exclusive rights to show all the Games, Summer and Winter, requested that the athletic, basketball, gymnastics, and swimming events in Beijing 2008 be rescheduled so that they could be shown live on US prime time between 6 pm and 9 pm. The IOC agreed to reschedule the gymnastics and swimming events.

While the Summer Games are a global television event, apart from the opening and closing ceremonies, different national audiences tend to see different Games. I was acutely reminded of this during the Athens Games of 2004 when for one week I was in the UK and the other I was in the United States. While in the UK, I was rewarded with hours of badminton, as British competitors slogged their way through the various rounds of the mixed doubles. The event was not shown in the United States. Television coverage reflects national sporting cultures and is tailored to promote national pride. Fencing is given massive coverage in Italy, whereas swimming, gymnastics, and track and field dominate US coverage. The "global" event of the Olympics is, in fact, a complex intersection of international and national media markets and audiences.

The LA Games of 1984 marked a permanent change in the size and source of revenues. Broadcasting rights and corporate sponsorship are now the major sources of revenue. However, the LA Games, unique in the recent history of the Games, had very strict control of expenditures. With no new buildings, limited infrastructural provisions, and the USOC responsible for any cost overruns, the LA Games increased revenue and limited costs. Subsequent Games in contrast, while they adopted the new revenue model, did not adopt the austere cost model. So, as revenues increased, so did costs. A lot.

The IOC and the financing of the games

Because IOC revenues have increased, there should be no problem in financing the Games. Right? The answer is no. Only some of the vast and burgeoning IOC revenues go toward paying for the Games. This raises two questions: Where do the IOC revenues go? and how are the Games financed?

The IOC uses its vast and burgeoning revenue to build up their own organization and promote Olympic sports. They use only around 40 percent to directly support the Games. Between 2001 and 2012, the IOC pulled in more than $9 billion in revenues from broadcasting rights, corporate sponsorship, and licensing. They keep 10 percent of all revenues for what they describe in their literature as 'operational and administrative costs.' For the 2001–2012 period, this amounted to almost $1 billion. With its location in tax-haven Switzerland and its status as a nonprofit organization, the IOC is an untaxed and largely opaque concentration of wealth and influence. With brimming coffers, the IOC is able to expand its own institutional footprint, ramp up self-promotion, and metastasize, like an aggressive cancer, into a significant economic force in world sports.

Some of the IOC revenues are directed toward the promotion of Olympic sports through revenue-sharing with NOCs and with International Federation of Olympic Sports. For the period 2001 to 2012, the IOC dispensed $1.69 billion to NOCs and $1.7 billion to the various international federations of Olympic sports. These monies help to promote Olympic sports, but they also solidify IOC influence. Only a few NOCs, from rich countries such as the USA and UK, can generate significant revenues on their own, and even fewer international federations. FIFA, the governing body of international soccer, is one of the few federations with sufficient funds to operate without IOC support. FIFA may have money but it does face an ethics deficit. Most international sport federations are heavily dependent on IOC support.

With this financial dispensation also comes considerable power. NOCs and international federations are unlikely to criticize the IOC. Organizations that could be more critical, and perhaps should be, are effectively muzzled by the simple fact that they receive a significant proportion of their funding from the IOC. This is especially true for the large number of NOCs from poorer countries, or the many international federations with little opportunity or ability to raise money on their own. By controlling the purse strings, the IOC wields effective power over the national and international sports organizations it profits from. The IOC conduit of cash also empowers IOC representatives. In many countries, the IOC is the main form of cash for sports. Becoming an IOC member is a sure route to the exercise of considerable power in a country's sports development. Becoming an IOC member also creates opportunities for directing the destination of IOC funds. In countries around the world, being connected with the IOC is a good way to get connected with serious cash.

Through the dispensing of vast revenues to NOCs and international federations, the IOC is like a wealthy client-state able to ensure loyalty and muzzle criticism from national Olympics organizations and international sports federations.

Less than 40 percent of all IOC revenue goes toward defraying the cost of hosting the Olympic Games. Table 3.1 summarizes the difference between estimates of the cost of recent Games and the IOC contribution. These data do not include infrastructure spending, which is often the largest component of total costs.

There is a difference between the direct cost of organizing the Games (which includes security, for example, and stadia), and the cost of hosting the Games (which includes wider infrastructural costs). The IOC does not include these latter costs, which allows them and the local organizing committees to hide the real costs of hosting the Games. I discuss the breakdown of direct and indirect infrastructure costs more fully in chapters 5 and 6.

Note that Table 3.1 mashes together two separate studies. While both use the US$ as their metric, they employ different inflation adjustments and assessments of costs. The Oxford study errs on the underestimation of costs. So, the two columns do not provide a perfect match and are best used as a rough-and-ready guide. But even this imprecise comparative data and underestimation of costs indicates that the IOC covers only a small proportion of the costs. The IOC provides less than 13 percent of the direct cost of the Games. The Games cost a great deal of money, but only a very small amount is provided by the IOC.

Table 3.1 The cost of Games

Games	Direct Cost of Games*	IOC Contribution**
Sochi	21.8	0.83
London	10.4	1.37
Vancouver	1.7	0.75
Beijing	6.8	1.25
Turin	4.3	0.56
Athens	2.9	0.96
Salt Lake City	2.5	0.55
Total	*50.4*	*6.27*

* Estimate by Oxford Olympic Study
** Olympic Marketing File
All figures in current US $billions

Let's summarize by looking at one recent Summer and Winter Games. For the 2012 Summer London and 2010 Winter Vancouver Games, the IOC received $950 million under the TOP program and $3.8 billion million for the broadcasting rights. With additional licensing fees, the total IOC revenue was $4.97 billion. The IOC gave $1.37 billion for London and $775 million for Vancouver. However, the London Games cost $18 billion, and the Vancouver Games cost $2.54 billion, for a combined cost of $17.44 billion but a combined IOC contribution of only $2.14 billion.

The IOC diverted some if its revenue toward promoting the NOCs ($735 million) and the various International Sports Federations ($729 million). For those doing the math, that still leaves $1.35 billion swallowed up by the IOC and rounding errors because the fiscal years do not align with the IOC quadrennial. The accountancy is not precise but what is clear is that the IOC uses a great deal of money to support itself, and gives some support to NOCs and international sports federations. Less than half of the money it takes in from the corporate sponsors and broadcasting rights is used to pay for the Games.

So, what makes up the gap between the cost of the Games and the IOC contribution? The individual organizing committee referred to as the Organizing Committee of the Olympic Games (OCOG) effectively runs each Games. The OCOG is in charge of running the Games in specific cities. Its executive members include IOC members of the host country, members of the National Olympic Committee (NOC) of the country hosting the Games, at least one member representing the host city, and local and national leaders, drawn from what the British call the 'great and the good.' The OCOG actually runs the show. The OCOG of Vancouver consisted of 20 members nominated by the NOC, the City of Vancouver, the Government of Canada, and assorted worthies.

The OCOGs are the bodies established to host and run specific Games. They receive money from the IOC, ticket sales, local licensing, and from domestic sponsorship programs for marketing rights within the host country. For Vancouver, this amounted to $688 million, for Sochi this amounted to $1.18 billion, and for London it was $1.15 billion. They are the same magnitudes as the IOC contribution for each of the Games but still nowhere near enough to self-finance the Games.

We need to note that all the costs, both official and unofficial, are estimates and should be treated with extreme caution. One of the dirty little secrets of the cost of the Games is that we are not quite sure of the real and total costs. With this huge this caveat in mind, we can still conclude that the main problem of the modern Games is that the direct revenues do not meet the actual costs of hosting the Games. So why do cities bid to host the Games? Let's look at this in more detail.

Notes

1 Renson, R. and den Hollander, M. (1997) Sport and business in the city: The Antwerp Olympic Games of 1920 and the urban elite. *Olympika* VI: 73–84. Quotes are from pp. 74 and 81.
2 Jonas, A. E. and Wilson, D. (1999) *The Urban Growth Machine: Critical Perspectives, Two Decades Later*. Albany: SUNY Press.
   Molotch, H. (1976) The city as a growth machine: Toward a political economy of place. *American Journal of Sociology* 82: 309–332.
3 IOC (International Olympic Committee) (2007) *The Top Program*. Geneva: IOC.

4   Bidding

"And the winner is . . ."

At a ceremony that captures global attention every two years, the president of the International Olympic Committee (IOC) begins with this phrase to announce the winning bid to host the Olympic Games in seven years. To take just one example: At a ceremony that began at 7:30 a.m. (local Singapore time) on July 6, 2005, the president of the International Olympic Committee (IOC) announced the winning bid to host the 2012 Summer Olympic Games. The five finalists – London, Madrid, Moscow, New York, and Paris – were narrowed down in four rounds of voting to two, Paris and London. Jacques Rogge, in a message carried live around the world, named London the winner. In Trafalgar Square, in the heart of London, jubilant Londoners celebrated the victory, while stunned Parisians gathering outside the City Hall openly wept.[1]

The bidding process

In the immediate post-WWII era it was US cities that, because they had the resources and had avoided war-related damage, dominated the pool of candidate cities. Of the seven candidate cities for the 1952 Olympics, five were US cities: Chicago, Detroit, Los Angeles, Minneapolis, and Philadelphia. Detroit was a candidate six times from 1952 to 1972.

As the costs of the Games escalated and revenues stagnated, the number of candidate cities dropped off. Fewer cities were eager to take on the financial burden. There were only four candidate cities for the Summer Games in 1964, 1968, and 1972; three for 1976; two for 1980; and only one for 1984. The financial success of Los Angeles, however, inaugurated a new era of intense city competition to host the Olympic Games. Globalization, now picking up pace, also played a role, as cities now competed more fiercely for an increasingly mobile capital. As the world flattened, investments travelled the world looking for the best returns. Hosting the Games was seen as a way to promote and enhance global standing.

After the 1984 Games, the number of candidate cities increased. Six cities bid for the 1992 Summer Games, including Amsterdam, Barcelona, Belgrade, Birmingham UK, Brisbane, and Paris. Bids now come from cities outside of Western Europe and North America. Since 2000, this include cities such as Cape Town, Baku, Bangkok, Buenos Aires, Doha, Havana, Rio, Osaka, Sydney, Beijing, and Istanbul. Some cities bid multiple times. Toronto unsuccessfully bid to host the 1960, 1964, 1976, 1996, and 2008 Games.

Since 1999, bidding for the Games is a complex process. Cities selected by their NOCs make a formal bid and fill in a questionnaire. At this stage, they are considered applicant cities. The IOC Executive Board then chooses cities from this list of applicants to proceed to the next stage, the candidate stage. Candidate cities must then submit an extended detailed questionnaire. Members of the IOC Evaluation Committee then make a site visit to each candidate city and report their findings to the IOC full committee. The city that achieves a simple majority of votes of the full IOC, sometimes after successive rounds of voting, is declared the host city and signs a bidding contract with the IOC.

Let's look at the competitive process to host the 2012 and 2020 Summer Games.

The competitive process to host the 2012 Summer Games began with a formal request in May 2003 by the IOC for NOCs to submit a city. All applicant cities had to submit a fee of $150,000 by August 2003. The nine nominated cities – Havana, Istanbul, Leipzig, London, Madrid, Moscow, New York, Paris, and Rio de Janeiro – then had to reply to an IOC questionnaire asking about the long-term impact and legacy of hosting the Games, the Games' place in the long-term planning of the city, the level of public and government support, the existing and planned sporting infrastructure, and the environmental impact of the Games. Based on the responses, the IOC drew up a short list of candidate cities in May 2004 that included London, Madrid, Moscow, New York, and Paris. These cities then had to submit a more-extensive three-volume bid book by November 2004. Each of the short-listed cities then received a formal three-day visit in February–March 2005. The IOC took a final vote in July 2005 in Singapore that led to joy in London and despair in Paris. Making a serious bid is an expensive proposition. The successful London bid cost $25 million.

In May 2011, the IOC invited NOCs to submit bids to host the 2020 Summer Games. By the deadline of September 2011, six bids had been received. The Italian NOC submitted Rome, but the city withdrew its bid before the applicant files were due. In May 2012, after viewing the applicant city files, the IOC selected three candidate cities: Tokyo, Istanbul, and Madrid. These three cities then had to submit more-detailed applications. In March 2013, the IOC Evaluation Commissions made a site visit to all three cities and on the basis of their reports, the full IOC in September 2013 selected Tokyo after a run-off in the second round between Tokyo and Istanbul.

Although the number of candidate cities has increased over the past 20 years, not all cities make it to the final rounds of IOC deliberations. As the Games become more elaborate and more expensive, with a greater reliance on already-existing substantial urban and sporting infrastructure, many cities in small and/or poor countries find it difficult to make it past the early rounds. Witness the early rejection of Havana for the 2008 and 2012 Games, and the fate of Baku compared to Chicago or Tokyo in the bidding process for the 2016 Games. Because of the heavy infrastructural requirements of hosting such a large international event, it is only the larger and richer cities that are now serious candidates to host the Summer Olympics. And while the refurbishment of existing venues rather than the building of new venues does limits costs, it also has the effect of limiting successful and viable bids to large, relatively wealthy cities that already have a substantial sports infrastructure. The possibility of cities from poor developing countries with limited existing facilities hosting the Games is rapidly diminishing in this new era.

Financial ability to host the Games and commercial "spin-off" (i.e., the ability to use the Games to penetrate new markets) are principal considerations for the IOC. Beijing was almost certain to win, given the willingness of the Chinese government to fund the Games and the huge commercial potential of the Chinese market for corporate sponsors.

Candidate cities now include global cities at the apex of the global urban hierarchy. Major cities such as New York, London, and Paris compete to host the Olympics and NOCs now increasingly promote the larger cities as their candidate cities. Small cities or cities from poor countries are at a great disadvantage in being applicant, and especially candidate, cities.

Because each country can have only one applicant city, larger, richer countries often have an internal competition. The competition for the US bid for the 2012 Games began in 1997 with eight cities – Cincinnati, Dallas, Houston, Los Angeles, New York, San Francisco, Tampa, and Washington-Baltimore. The USOC dropped Cincinnati, Dallas, and Los Angeles from consideration. In February 2002, only four cities made the cut: Houston, New York, San Francisco, and Washington-Baltimore. In November 2002, the decision came down to New York and San Francisco. New York was selected. The city's global recognition was an important factor. The USOC eliminated Houston from the final consideration because of 'poor international recognition.' Houston's failed bid to host the 2012 Games is a salutary reminder of a city's limitations. The USOC rejected the bid because the city did not have a high enough international profile. I will refer to this as the 'Houston paradox.' In other words, the very cities that are desperate to host

Figure 4.1 An Olympic sign in Salt Lake City, Utah. The bid for these 2002 Winter
Games was revealed as morally bankrupt and financially corrupt

Source: John Rennie Short

the Games, because they are in the wannabe global city category, are the ones most likely to fail. The British OC proposed Manchester for the 1996 and 2000 Games but was only successful when it put forward London as its candidate city for the 2012 Games.

Bidding scandals

Bidding for the Winter Games follows a procedure similar to the Summer Games after the scandal of the Salt Lake City bid. The city was desperate to host the Winter Games. It made bids to host the 1932, 1972, 1976 (the USOC chose Denver), and 1992 Games (the USOC chose Anchorage, Alaska). Hosting the Winter Games would give some form of global recognition to the city, the state, and the Mormon Church (Church of the Latter-Day Saints), an influential player in the politics of the state and city. From 1986 to 1996, the city's bid committee worked the IOC and the various international sporting federations, making their case. The city's bid team was convinced that they needed to be very generous to IOC members. They drew on the experience of Nagano that spent, at the very least, $20 million on hosting 62 IOC members. That bid was successful and Nagano hosted the 1998 Games.

Each member of the IOC was personally invited to visit Salt Lake City. Seventy took up the offer. The bid committee, as we now know from various account and reports, effectively bribed IOC members to vote for the city. The bribes were in the form of direct payments, tuition payments, 'charitable' donations, and land purchase deals.[2]

Before the reforms in the wake of the Salt Lake City scandal, IOC delegates would visit bid cities, ostensibly to check out the site, and then vote in a secret ballot. Each IOC member held an all-important vote that they could cast in secret. Cities were lavish with their hospitality, and many delegates were eager to cash in on their voting power. All IOC members who visited bid cities were wined and dined, and some were bought and paid for in return for their vote. There were no IOC checks on members visiting the cities or ethical guidelines in place. Bid authorities constructed dossiers of IOC members that highlighted their weaknesses. The dossier prepared for Stockholm's bid for the 2004 Summer Olympics noted that Mohammed Mzali of Tunisia 'should always be taken out for dinner on visits to Paris,' while General Gadir of Sudan is 'known for appreciating delicious food and drinking.'[3] The system led to delegates leveraging more and more lavish gifts from cities' boosters who were increasingly eager to lubricate their bid with generous 'hospitality.' One IOC member was routinely referred to as the 'human vacuum cleaner' for his ability to suck up money, gifts, holidays, flights, and medical attention for himself and his family.

The scandal unfolded when it was revealed by a television station in Salt Lake City in November 1998 that the city's bid committee had paid for an IOC member's daughter to attend a private university in the United States. The next month, a Swiss IOC member, Marc Hodler, stated in public that he believed that there was 'massive corruption,' and that as many as 25 IOC members had had their votes bought. An IOC Commission was quickly formed in response to media pressure and especially to the worries of corporate sponsors that their products would be tainted with the label of corruption. The commission reported in 1999 that seven IOC members were to be expelled, including Jean-Claude Ganga of the Congo, General Gadir of Sudan, Sergio Fantani of Chile, and Augustin Arroyo of Ecuador. Ten more IOC members were warned about their behavior, two were exonerated. The scandal brought the scrutiny of media attention to the lavish life style of IOC members who, it was revealed for the first time, were given business-class flights to the Games and full-time drivers and luxury cars during their stays. They were installed in luxury accommodations with specific requirements for fresh flowers to be placed in their rooms each day of their residence. These requirements were in deep contrast to the more Spartan accommodations and basic conditions afforded to the athletes of the Games. The penchant for President Samaranch to be referred to as 'His Excellency' was symptomatic of an unelected, unaccountable para-state grown heavy and fat with excessive entitlements. The IOC members expected and were granted the privileged lifestyle of the global elite.

After the investigations were complete, 10 members were out of the IOC – six were expelled and four resigned – and another 10 were sanctioned. In the wake of the Salt Lake scandal, the IOC created an Ethics Committee and made changes to the bid process. In 1999, a new procedure was set up in which the guiding principle was, in the words of the IOC, 'no visits, no gifts.' Only an evaluation committee, not the full IOC, was involved in site visits, although all IOC members still made the final decision. This directive was less concerned with democratizing the process or even making it more transparent; it was essentially a response to the bad publicity and the fear of corporate withdrawal. As the head of McDonald's German subsidiary noted, "If the corruption suspicions are confirmed, McDonald's will ask itself if sponsorship of the Games still has a place on the group's image."[4] In the immediate aftermath of the scandal, corporate sponsors put pressure on the IOC to clean up their act.

The bidding process still gives power to members of the IOC who can vote and influence the vote of others. Bid committees of candidate cities try to influence the voting, sometimes simply through the force of their arguments about hosting a wonderful event, but also through their generosity toward IOC voters. But there is a fine line between legitimate generosity – wining and dining, gifts and entertainment – and the more-dubious forms of consultancy fees and third-party payments.

Desperate cities meet powerful voters. It is a recipe for corruption. While the reforms of 1999 and subsequent tweaks have eradicated the more-obvious instances of vote buying, it still continues. Doha was disqualified to host the 2016 Games after allegations of attempted bribery of IOC members. And for a more recent example: consider the case of Frank Fredericks, a former Olympic athlete from Namibia who became an IOC member and was a member of the executive board from 2008 to 2012. He was member of the evaluation committee for the 2012 and 2020 Games. In 2017, it was revealed that he was paid almost $300,000 in 2009 on the very day after Rio was awarded the 2016 Games. He resigned from his position as chair of the evaluation committee for the 2024 Games. The Japanese Olympic Committee is also investigating allegations that the bid committee for Tokyo paid bribes in order to host the Games in 2020. The beat of corruption goes on.[5]

The pernicious effects of bidding

Because the IOC owns the rights to the Olympic Games, the bidding process gives the IOC more power to make demands. Bid cities have to underwrite the costs, guarantee government support, ensure public support, and be aware of the environmental impacts. To what extent all these various demands are actually met is moot. Sochi was an environmental disaster despite the environmentally sensitive bid and the IOC formal commitment to greening the Games.

The bidding process guarantees the IOC continued power and leverage. Any attempt to change comes up against the IOC insistence on the circulating host city model. The creation of a permanent site or a smaller number of regular sites would reduce the bargaining ability, and ultimately the financial power, of the IOC. The IOC prefers the current model for the simple reason that the status quo reinforces its power and bargaining ability.

Why do cities bid?

Given the disparity in the bargaining position between the IOC and potential host cities, the question then arises, why do cities bid to host the Games? There are many reasons why an individual city may bid. The IOC alleges a number of benefits of hosting. Let us consider some of the more important ones.

Bidding as national redemption

Sometimes, a bid is an attempt to reposition the host country in a new light. The Olympic Games allows countries to attempt to rebrand themselves in the international imagination. Former Axis powers cemented their postwar international citizenship by hosting Games: Rome and Tokyo in 1960 and 1964, and West Germany in 1972. Hosting the Games can reestablish international credibility and rehabilitate national reputations. Sins can be washed out with an Olympic cleansing.

The Games also provide an opportunity for new and emergent countries and cities to reconnect with the global community with a new image. The 1988 Seoul Games were used by the South Korean government to open the society up to the global community. Hosting the 1988 Summer Games gave a stamp of international approval to an emergent power. The Barcelona Games of 1992 allowed the Catalonia of a post-Franco Spain to be shown to the world. And the 2001 awarding of the 2008 Games to Beijing, along with China's entry into the World Trade Organization, marked the culmination of China's growing international involvement and global citizenship. The Sochi Winter Games of 2014 allowed the presentation of a more-upbeat and affluent Russia after the misery of the 1990s. Rio's hosting of the Games in 2016 was a way to show a democratic and increasingly affluent Brazil to the rest of the world.

While participation in the Games is used to promote national prestige, they can also become the stage for more complex issues of national representation. Hosting the Games can also allow the opportunities for different nations of a state to be represented. In the 1992 Games in Barcelona, for example, Catalan nationalism was an important part of the rhetoric of the Games. The Catalan national anthem was played at the opening ceremony, and both Catalan and Spanish nationalisms were employed in the Games. In a mutually beneficial compromise between different parts of the nation-state, Catalan sensitivities were embodied into the Games, while Spain was presented as a modern, liberal, pluralist democracy. The success of the Barcelona Games was in part the "win-win-win" of the three scales of nation, state, and city. Spain enhanced its reputation as an efficient democracy, Catalonia got an economic boost and a sense of identity in the wider world, and Barcelona received an urban makeover and improvements in its infrastructure and global connections.

And we should never forget simple vanity. The major political players get to strut the world stage, albeit briefly, if their city hosts the Games.

The urban growth machine

There are business groups within cities that want to host the Games. City elites, who promote the economic competitiveness of the city through attracting investment and spurring economic growth, are the urban growth machine. It consists of local business elites, including developers, construction companies, the tourist industry, and their political supporters who work to promote the hosting of events. The Games are a great opportunity to increase business, generate revenues, and enhance profits. City elites have long used the Games in urban boosterism. The elite of Antwerp used the 1920 Games to advance their own economic agenda. And from Atlanta to Vancouver, business interests and their political allies work to promote the hosting of events. And there are few business opportunities like the Olympic Games with its promise of vast building programs and massive public spending. The Games is a huge trough of business opportunities.

Across the world, city elites are promoting a global city imaginary; a vision of a self-consciously 'global' city replete with images of busy international airports, foreign tourists, and upgraded infrastructure. Elites and urban political regimes call on this imaginary to generate public support for projects, to justify tax incentives, and business friendly policies. Bidding and hosting the Games and other international mega-events is a central theme in this discourse. Hosting the Games is winning the gold medal of global inter-city competition.

Global attention

Guy Debord coined the phrase "society of the spectacle," asserting that the spectacle is the chief product of present-day society.[6] The commodification of actual experience creates impersonal spectacles, which are witnessed rather than experienced. Arguably, some of the most important spectacles are sports mega-events, such as the Olympic Games, which reach a worldwide television audience and offer perhaps the best stage upon which a city can make the claim to global status.

The dazzling opening ceremonies of the Olympics provide the platform for immediate global recognition. The subsequent coverage of sporting events provides an unsurpassed media spectacle focused on a distinct urban setting. This promise of worldwide exposure and economic gain makes hosting the Games a major goal for many aspiring city elites around the world. It provides an opportunity for city re-imaginings as well as re-makings. In the context of a global media spotlight, the spectacular staging of the Games becomes the setting for a dramaturgical remaking and representation of the city. The Games allow a city to showcase itself to a global audience and become more globally connected. For two weeks, the city is constantly mentioned and represented in the world's media. Hosting the Games allows the city to achieve global recognition, with the possibility of increased tourism and investment.

A positive image is maintained only with the hosting of a success Games. The Munich Games are remembered as the site of terrorist attack. Atlanta is recalled for a bombing as well as for crass commercialism. And the delays in the final completion of the Athens Games reinforced negative stereotypes of

Greek inefficiency. The Beijing Games conjured up images of spectacular stadia and well-run events, but they also provided images of an authoritarian regime as well as reminders of the appalling air quality in Beijing. The coverage of the Sochi Games often became an opportunity for criticism of an authoritarian Russia. The image of Brazil and Rio was as much damaged as enhanced by hosting the 2016 Games. To host the Game is to open the city to intense scrutiny and spectacular failure.

Urban makeovers

City elites bid to host the Games because getting ready to host the Games provides an opportunity for massive urban renewal, major environmental remediation, dramatic infrastructural improvements, and the creation of a positive image across the globe. The Games allow the construction of a global city and the making of a modern city.

Hosting the Games in this contemporary era involves a massive urban transformation, including the provision of venues and major infrastructural investment. The Games start on a specific date with a global audience. The brute reality of such a severe deadline overcomes political resistances, bureaucratic logjams, and administrative inertia.

Selling the bid

Successful bids need to be sold by the organizing committees to the local communities. The IOC now requires that candidate cities indicate a high level of popular support for the city's application.

Backers of the Games routinely evoke feelings of community as well as intense nationalism and civic pride. The Games have a strong positive image. In a time of frayed and fraying civic connections, bidding for and hosting the Games holds both the promise and reality of creating a sense of solidarity, a feeling of communal ownership of the event, and a collective goodwill during and immediately after the Games. The Games can tap into large reservoirs of civic pride and deep feelings of urban community. The bid, and the prospect of hosting the Games, provides a celebratory framework that can generate substantial popular as well as business support.

But the huge costs and massive disruption of hosting the Games can pose serious issues for city elites hoping to promote a candidate city. However, three things aid in the selling of the Games. The first is the combined economic and political weight of the urban growth machine. The Games provide such a huge development potential that urban growth machines mobilize all their powers of influence and persuasion. There is often an asymmetry in power and resources between urban elites and local opposition.

The second, folded into the first, is the overestimation of benefits and the underestimation of costs. The large and growing indirect costs of infrastructure provision are rarely included in the official estimates of costs. There is an intentional low-balling of bids and the generation of cost-benefit analyses more sensitive to benefits than costs: more of this in a subsequent chapter when we look into the costs and benefits in more detail.

Third, arguments favoring the hosting of the Games can also draw upon the recent positive experience of host cities. The Olympic Games do provide some economic benefits to the city as a whole because they accelerate projects already in the pipeline, force national and state urban expenditures, and mobilize public spending that may remain blocked without the deadline of an opening ceremony to a global media audience.

Opposing the bid

Bids rely on local support. The IOC needs to be assured that it is awarding the Games to a city that wants it and is willing to pay for it. But as costs mount and benefits prove more illusory, there is mounting resistance to bids.

There is long history of local resistance to Olympics bids. The USOC picked Denver to bid for the 1976 Winter Olympics, but after two local referenda the idea was vetoed, so Innsbruck, that had just hosted in 1964, was given the nod. Amsterdam's bid for the 1992 Games was vigorously opposed by a powerful coalition of left wing activists and the squatters' movement. This Nolympics movement, as it called itself, organized an event where IOC officials were pelted with fruit and eggs before they boarded a boat for a trip through the city canals. No surprise then that the 1992 Olympics went to Barcelona.

Berlin's bid for the 2000 Games led to a widespread campaign that involved demonstrations, vandalism, and graffiti. Visiting IOC delegates needed the protection of 1,500 police officers. The Games were awarded to Sydney, where there was widespread support but also a significant anti-Games movement. One organization, Rentwatchers, part of a broad coalition known as the Anti-Olympic Alliance, carefully tracked rent increases in the housing market.

The Bread Not Circus group campaigned against Toronto's bid to host the 2008 Games and gave a presentation to the visiting IOC delegation. There were other factors at work but the IOC awarded the 2008 Games to Beijing.

There is resistance to every Olympics bid. The Games are disruptive enough that protests will be mounted. Vancouver's bid for the 2010 Winter Games sparked protest from First Nations, environmentalists, and social activists in the city. Despite their protests, the bid went ahead and the city hosted the 2010 event.

But in recent years, more people think the Games are a bad idea. Resistance to hosting the Games is growing, widening, and deepening such that there is a draining of support in the wider community for the idea of bidding for the Games. With more publicity afforded to the costs of hosting the Games, more local communities are leery of letting their city become a bid or host city. The disruption and displacement, the high costs, and dubious benefits of previous Games now feed into growing oppositional movements. There are many who consider that hosting the Games will lead to "pathologies of murky tendering: price gouging, graft and gigantic cost overruns."[7]

Sometimes, the protest is enough to sink a city's bid at the very early stages. In 2015, the mayor of Toronto decided not to even put the city's name forward as an applicant city to host the 2024 Games. Although some on the City Council and the Canadian Olympic Committee supported the bid, there was a distinct lack of business and political support in the city as a whole.

Opposition is more muted in nondemocratic and authoritarian societies, so the most-successful resistances are found in the more-democratic societies. The bidding for the 2022 Winter Games is instructive in this regard.

There were some early dropouts. After its failure to get the 2018 Games, Munich in Germany considered bidding again for the 2022 Games, but the plan was scuttled in 2013 when a majority of residents voted against the idea, citing fiscal and environmental costs. St. Moritz/Davos in Switzerland also considered bidding as early as 2011, but the proposal was undermined by the result of a plebiscite held in 2013.

By 2015, there were six bid cities: Beijing, Almaty, Krakow, Lviv, Oslo, and Stockholm. Lviv's bid was cancelled due to the crisis in Ukraine 2013–15. Understandable, given that the country was in political crisis and armed conflict. The other withdrawals, in contrast, were due to lack of support.

Stockholm cancelled its bid in 2013 because of lack of political support. Krakow's bid was undermined by a local referendum. In 2013, the Norwegian OC submitted a bid but in a series of polls, support never reached more than 37 percent approval rates. Public scrutiny of the IOC 700-page document listing various demands for host cities undermined Norwegians' appetite for hosting the Games. So, the effective bids came down to Almaty in Kazakhstan and Beijing. In effect, the choice came down to two countries, neither noted for their history of winter sports, human rights, or their democratic accountability.

At a full meeting of IOC meeting in Kuala Lumpur in 2015, Beijing won out over Almaty. The Chinese message at this final meeting before the election was that that China would protect the long-term financial viability of the Games. In other words, no matter the cost of the IOC demands, China would pay.

It was similar story for the 2024 Summer Games. Toronto dropped out at the very early stages. In 2014, the USOC selected Boston as the US bid for host the 2024 Games, beating out Los Angeles, San Francisco, and Washington, DC. Very quickly, a No Boston Olympics movement began to mobilize. Public support for the bid dwindled after the public disclosure of the possibility of a half-billion-dollar shortfall. The Boston bid was undercut when the financial costs were revealed and there was growing awareness of possibility of cost overruns and long-term debt. In 2015, Boston's bid was officially terminated and Los Angeles because the US official bid city.

Budapest, Hamburg, and Rome also were candidate cities to host the 2024 Games. However, all fell by the wayside due to local opposition. Hamburg was the choice of the German OC. The city revised its previous bid for the 2012 Games. This is common occurrence. It takes lot of time and effort to put in a serious bid, and many cities recycle their bids in subsequent years, tweaking and retooling. Rio bid for the 2004 and 2012 Games before finally snagging the 2016 Games. Tokyo bid for the 2016 Games before winning the competition to host the 2020 Games. Paris bid for the 2008, 2012, and 2024 Games. Hamburg's second bid was scuttled by a referendum vote in November 2015, when close to 52 percent of voters in the city rejected the bid. The opposition voters stressed the financial burdens of the IOC, the environmental damage, and the opportunity costs.

In 2016, the mayor of Rome withdrew the bid because it lacked the support of the city government, fearful of the costs and possibility of carrying a huge debt. In the case of Budapest, when an opposition movement got enough votes to trigger a referendum, the organizing committee withdrew the bid in February 2016.

The critics of all these failed bids pointed to corruption, government money spent on Games rather than on health and education, and even the fact that infrastructure improvements could be better targeted for residents rather than just for two-week visitors.

So, the Games may have a harder time in the future generating enough support in affluent democratic societies. When a city's bid is open to democratic accountability and more-transparent cost-benefit analysis, then public support can wither.

For the moment, there are enough cities around the world that want to host the Games. But if the hosting moves into less-affluent countries or more-authoritarian societies, then the image of the Games may be tarnished; Sochi in 2014 and Rio in 2016 were Games with troubling images and unsettling implications. The final choice of the 2022 Winter Games ended up between the totalitarian and the authoritarian. Neither one builds a positive brand for the Olympics.

Losing as winning: the victory of unsuccessful bids

The real winners of the bid process may be the cities that put together a bid but fail to win. In 2009, it was announced that Rio was the winner of the competition to host the 2016 Summer Games. The announcement was celebrated in Brazil, while sadness reigned in Chicago. President Obama perhaps second-guessed his decision to be the first US president to lobby in person for a US Olympics bid. But the real winners may be the cities like Chicago that just failed to win the final nomination. The bid application can involve a reimagining of the city, an opportunity plan for a greener, fairer, more efficient city. A bid has to consider the long-term plans for the city and its environmental footprint and access to public sports facilities. For the price of a bid ,a city can use the exercise to visualize and plan for a better city. So, the winners may not be the cities that get to host the Games with all their attendant costs and headaches, but those that used the bid to reimagine the city. Cities with unsuccessful bids get to dream of making a better city but without the heavy costs of actually hosting the Olympics.

There is a lucrative ecosystem of bid consultants and professional firms that advise cities in making bids. The average cost of bids is around $31 million, although the largest was roughly $89 million for Tokyo's successful bid to host the 2020 Games. A lot of money, especially if the bid fails. But unsuccessful bids have an important role in a reimagining of the city. The Baltimore-Washington bid for the 2012 Games failed in the early US rounds. A central theme of the bid was the remediation of the Anacostia River. Popular support was mobilized and this did decline, but did not disappear after the bid's rejection. Even unsuccessful bids can generate new ways of imagining a city.

In 1991, Stockholm put in a bid to host the 2004 Games. The application envisioned the makeover of a brown field site on the Hammarby waterfront area as the Olympic Village. The bid was unsuccessful but did stimulate the redevelopment of Hammarby from 1993 as a showpiece of ecologically sensitive urban planning. The city purchased the land and set about building a community with closed loops of water, waste and energy circulation, solar panels, and lots of green spaces.

Some bids may even stimulate wider social debates. The 1996 Toronto bid suggested post-event housing for low-income residents, union jobs, and environmental assessments. The Cape Town bid of 2004 started off as the usual development bid promoted by business elites, but after the election of the first democratically elected government in 1996, it emphasized human development and addressed urban inequalities rather than just the interests of financial capital, developers, and construction companies. The bid promoted construction in disadvantaged areas, venues supporting community sports, human resource development through jobs, community consultation, and an integrated transport system that linked the poorer, peripheral communities more fully into a metropolitan transport network.[8]

Even failed bids may act as a catalyst for new ways of think about a city, planning a city, and even reimagining a city. Putting ideas down on paper for an external audience allows creative space for images of a new better-organized, more-efficient, more-modern, and equitable city.

Serial bidders may be less concerned with hosting the Games than with using the bid process as a way to reimagine the city. Bids can be a vehicle for about how to refashion the city. And subsequent bids that are tweaked and changed become part of an internal debate. Serial bidding can be a valuable learning process. Istanbul has, so far, failed five times to host the Games, in 2000, 2004, 20008, 2012, and 2020, but the bidding embodies the international impulses and global aspirations of the city elite. Cities can recycle the bids for hosting other sport events. Toronto's 1996 and 2008 Olympics bidding laid the basis for its successful 2015 Pan American Games. Manchester UK's 1996 and 2000 bids laid the basis for the 2002 Commonwealth Games.

There is also a post-bid legacy, even for the failed bids. NYC's bid for 2012 made in 2005 emphasized seven undeveloped areas of the city. The NYC2012 plan called for construction of new stadiums, transportation improvements, and environmental clean-up efforts. Although London was ultimately selected to host the 2012 summer games, it is claimed by some that the NYC2012 plan helped to catalyze longstanding infrastructure and development projects in New York, such as the construction of a housing project in Queens, the extension of the No. 7 subway line, a subway extension, new sports stadium, and new parks.[9] It is, of course, difficult to measure the exact degree to which the bid influenced subsequent developments, but it is clear that it did not hinder them, and articulating them and planning for them allowed space and oxygen for the subsequent changes to take place.

We know that hosting the Olympic Games causes changes in cities. But failed bids also have the possibility of generating new urban narratives and creating new urban structures. Focusing on bids that fail rather than just the winners that host extends our understanding of the Olympic Games.[10]

Notes

1 I draw heavily upon a previously published paper:
  Short, J. R. (2008) Globalization, cities and the Summer Olympics. *City* 12: 321–340.
2 Longman, J. (2000) Olympic: Leaders of Salt Lake City Olympic bid are indicted in bribery scandal. *The New York Times*. www.nytimes.com/2000/07/21/sports/olympics-leaders-of-salt-lake-olympic-bid-are-indicted-in-bribery-scandal.html
  Siddons, L. (1999) IOC expels six members in Salt Lake City scandal. *The Guardian*. www.theguardian.com/sport/1999/mar/17/ioc-expels-members-bribes-scandal

3 Calvert, J. (2002) How to buy the Olympics. *Observer Sport Monthly* 21: 32–37. Quotes are from p. 35.
4 Korporaal, G. and Evans, M. (1999) Games people play. *Sydney Morning Herald* 11: 2.
5 Wilson, S. (2016) The Olympics are having an unprecedented meltdown. *Business Insider*. www.businessinsider.com/the-olympics-are-having-an-unprecedented-meltdown-2016-5
6 Debord, G. (1967) *The Society of the Spectacle*. New York: Zone Books.
7 Goldblatt, D. (2016) *The Games: A Global History of the Olympics*. New York: W. W. Norton, p. 336.
8 Hiller, H. H. (2000) Mega-events, urban boosterism and growth strategies: An analysis of the objectives and legitimations of the Cape Town 2004 Olympic Bid. *International Journal of Urban and Regional Research* 24: 449–458.
9 Maurita (2012) NYC 2012: Imagining The Olympic Games in New York City. *From The Stacks: New York Historical Society*. http://blog.nyhistory.org/nyc-2012-imagining-the-olympic-games-in-new-york-city/ Accesses 8/29/17.
10 Olivier, R. and Lauermann, J. (2017) *Failed Olympic Bids and the Transformation of Urban Space*. London: Palgrave.

5 Rising costs

Over the past century, the Olympic Games have increased in size. As they become more gargantuan, they become more expensive and impose a larger urban footprint. Conservative estimates put the direct cost of hosting the last three Summer Games at $4.5 billion for Rio, $6.8 billion for Beijing, and $10.4 billion for London. Even the smaller Winter Games come with expensive price tags: $22 billion for Sochi, $1.7 billion for Vancouver, and $4.3 billion for Turin. And remember, these are just the direct costs.

We can make a distinction between different types of costs. There are two sets of direct costs: the operational costs incurred by the OCOG in hosting the Games, including security and the construction costs of building or refurbishing the venues that hold the events. There are also the indirect costs of getting a city ready to host the Games. These include the construction costs of new airports, roads, and rail and other infrastructural improvements. And there are the social and environmental costs of hosting the Games. Many studies and discussions elide these different types, making it difficult to make comparisons and assessment. In this chapter, I will try to keep them separate.

Expansion of direct costs

A number of factors drive up the direct costs. One is the sheer increase in the size of the Games. Today, there are more athletes than ever competing in more events in more sports. At the first modern Games in Athens in 1896, there were only 241 participants competing in 43 events in nine sports, with little press in attendance. By 2016 in Rio, there were over 11,000 athletes competing in a total of 306 medal events in 28 sports, reported on by more than 21,000 accredited media personnel from around the world.

The number of sports continues to increase. Previously, the IOC only needed a two-thirds majority for a sport to be included in the Games. Now only a simple majority of all IOC members is required. The pressure from

International Sports Federations to include their sport, as well as the constant demand to maintain and increase the size of the viewing public, has led to an increase in the number of sports and events.

Some of the increase in the number of athletes is due to increased gender equity in participation. But the IOC also adds new sports and events to the Games in order capture sports and events with widespread media and youth appeal. The Winter Games, for example, now includes events from sports that first emerged in the Winter X Games. An event with particular youth appeal, BMX riding, made its debut at the 2008 Summer Games. For the 2016 Games, two new sports were introduced, rugby sevens and golf. The rugby completion required its own stadium, while the golf tournament required the construction of a new golf course in a city and a country where golf is not a popular sport. There is even talk of a return of cricket to the Games, a game that was played only once before in the 1900 Games. For the 2018 Winter Games in Pyeonchang, athletes were able for the first time to compete in big air snowboarding and freestyle skiing, mass speed skating, and mixed doubles curling. Tokyo 2020 will see the addition of karate, sport climbing, skateboarding, and surfing.

While it is easy to add a new sport, it is more difficult to get rid of old sports and events, because they have constituencies of influence and power even if they may lack or lose media appeal. Archery or shooting is something I like to watch but lacks the mass appeal of the 100-meter dash or of watching fearless athletes doing acrobatics on the half pipe. Occasionally, some sports are dropped. Softball and baseball were dropped from the 2012 London Games. Part of the reason was that these sports were not universal, but the same could be said of golf. A deciding factor was that they required purpose-built stadia that increased the already escalating costs of hosting the Games. It was an easy decision for the IOC to make, but baseball will likely be added to Tokyo 2020. The IOC responds to two competing pressures: on the one hand, adding new sports and events in order to maintain and enhance its global monopoly of sports coverage and to keep attracting a young and fickle audience; on the other, trying to put a brake on the accelerating costs of the Games.

As new sports emerge and capture the much-desired youth market, the IOC tries to incorporate them. If an event such as BMX riding or snowboarding attracts a following and then an audience and then media attention, then it is ripe for IOC incorporation and inclusion in the Games. And the international federations of these emerging sports and events want the imprimatur of the IOC to legitimize and expand their sport. The IOC needs to maintain appeal and the new sports organizations want the global platform of the Olympic Games. So, while some sports may be dropped, the overall trend is for more sports and more events.

Compare the two Olympic Games in Athens. In 1896, Athens had to provide for only 241 participants competing in 43 events in nine sports. In 2004, the same city had to prepare for 11,000 athletes competing in 301 events in 28 sports. One stadium sufficed for most of the 1896 Games, but 108 years later in the same city, separate venues were needed for swimming, athletics, soccer, tennis, archery, rowing, sailing, kayaking, equestrian events, and many more.

In order to host the modern Summer Olympic Games in this new era, a city must provide a wide range of sports venues and arenas. As the Games increase in size, they make a larger impact on the host cities. Providing all the necessary venues cost Athens $2.9 billion. Beijing spent close to $6.8 billion on athletic venues, including the $428 million on the 91,000 seat Bird's Nest Stadium.

Thirty-three separate venues were required to host the 2016 Rio Games, including stadia for athletics, basketball, wrestling and judo, fencing and taekwondo, handball, one aquatics center for diving and water polo and another for swimming, a tennis center, a gymnastics hall, and a velodrome. Venues and facilities had to be built for rowing, yachting, showjumping and other equestrian events, dirt bike riding, and golf.

Figure 5.1 Direct costs: The Bird's Nest Stadium built for the 2008 Beijing Games at a cost of $428 million

Source: https://commons.wikimedia.org/wiki/File:Beijing_Birds_Nest_Closeup.jpg

The Games just get bigger and more expensive. Since 1960, the average Summer Games now cost $5.2 billion, while the Winter Games average out at $3.1 billion.

One way to contain costs is to use existing building rather than construct new ones. Many cities now refurbish stadiums as a way to limit costs. The Los Angeles, Seoul, Barcelona, and Athens Games all refurbished their main Olympic stadium. Table 5.1 shows the use of existing venues in the Athens Games of 2004. Even the Beijing Games, with its arresting and brand new Bird's Nest Stadium and glass cube of an aquatic center, relied heavily on exiting venues. Beijing built only 12 new venues, created eight temporary venues, and refurbished 11 others.

Table 5.1 Main athletic venues for the 2004 Athens Games

Venue	Land area in hectares
Olympic Stadium	12.7
Olympic Indoor Hall	6.1
Aquatic Center	7.8
Tennis Center	6.9
Velodrome	5.3
Soccer Stadium	**7.5**
Rowing and Canoeing	12.4
Sports Pavilion	**8.1**
Beach Volleyball	**12.3**
Volleyball Stadium	8.1
Judo and Wrestling Hall	6.5
Boxing Hall	**12.7**
Gymnastics and Table Tennis	9.5
Weightlifting Hall	0.8
Pentathlon Center	23.1
Baseball Stadium	**12.0**
Softball	**5.7**
Canoe-Kayak Center	28.8
Hockey Center	**11.5**
Sailing Center	**33.6**
Shooting Center	31.2
Equestrian Center	94.0
Total	356.6

Bold designates entirely new facilities; all others were fully renovated
Source: Calculated by author

New building is expensive, a fact dramatically revealed in the Sochi Games, by far the most expensive Winter Games and one of the most expensive Games ever, because a winter sports complex had to be constructed from scratch and new infrastructure built to connect the subtropical city to the venues in the mountains.

However, the reliance on an existing infrastructure limits the possibility of hosting the Game to cities that are either are very rich and can devote enormous resources, or have a substantial legacy of sporting venues.

Costs also escalate because the Olympic Games are the most-watched media event. The city and the country are in the global eye during the immediate build up and the scrutiny is intense during the two weeks of the Games. The host cities want to put on a good face to the external world and internal audiences.

The Olympic Games are the modern-day equivalent of the potlatch. At the potlatch ceremony in traditional societies of the Pacific Northwest, leaders gave away or destroyed valuable material objects in order to display wealth and enhance prestige. We can see the Olympic Games as an elaborate potlatch ceremony in which the host city provides dazzling opening ceremonies, signature buildings, and lavish facilities in order to enhance their prestige. It is a form of conspicuous construction in order to impress.

There is also a ratchet effect. The Beijing Games raised the bar on the scale and choreography of the opening ceremonies, and the Birds Nest Stadium and glass-cubed aquatics center were the ultimate in trophy-style buildings. While subsequent Games have yet to match the Beijing Games, their ceremonies set the standard. In order to achieve recognition and prestige, hosts have to make grand architectural statements and host spectacular opening ceremonies that come close to matching and ultimately surpassing the Beijing extravaganza. And they all come with a cost.

Security

There are also new direct costs. There is also the mounting level of security costs. As the most global of events, the Olympic Games are a prime target for terrorist attacks. Munich 1972 and Atlanta in 1996 witnessed kidnappings and bombings that increased security precautions. But after 9/11 and the possibility of a spectacular terrorist attack increased, security operations were ramped up. Athens employed 70,000 specially trained police and soldiers for the 2004 Games and spent more than eight times what Sydney 2000 spent on security. Security expenditure that amounted to $108 million for Atlanta 1996 and $179 million in Sydney 2000 escalated to $1.5 billion in Athens. The cost per athlete was respectively $10,486, $16,062, and $142,897.

One day after London was announced as the winner of the competition to host the 2012 Games, a terrorist bomb attack hit the city. The security budget for the Games was immediately increased from 225 million British pounds to one billion British pounds. It is difficult to estimate the real cost. Government subsidization through provision of military personnel and national and local police is considerable and probably unknowable. The London Games employed the British Army at the main Olympic site as a security force.

The security costs for Sochi were close to $2 billion, almost double the figure for the previous Vancouver games, and the estimated $1.6 billion for the London Games.

Cost overruns

Costs exceed initial estimates most of the time. A study of Summer Olympics from 1972 to 2008 found substantial differences between initial estimate and actual spending.[1] For Athens and Beijing, the actual costs were between three and four times the initial estimates. This finding is confirmed by another study of Winter and Summer Olympics from 1960 to 2012 that found that the real cost of the Games on average are 2.5 times the initial budget estimate.[2] This average hides tremendous variation, while London was 'only' 76 percent above estimate; Sochi was a whopping 289 percent. The general conclusion is that the Games always cost much more that the initial bid. The real costs consistently overrun the initial cost estimates. And they have more-consistent and higher overruns even compared with other megaprojects, such as motorways and new rail projects.

We can take a number of conclusions for these findings. The first is that the Games are always more expensive than initially estimated. There is persistent undercounting of costs in the initial bids. Since bids need public support and government intervention, there is a tendency to proffer the lowest possible estimates in order to hide the true financial cost. Low-ball bids help gain support. If the bid wins, the fiscal recriminations follow later.

There is also the other possibility that hosting the Games brings unavoidable costs, including delays, new security costs, and the unforeseen cost of creating a globally watched megaproject with a fixed start date. In order to finish project in time, more overtime has to be worked, more incentives have to be paid, and so the cost keeps mounting. The bids are always low-ball figures in order to ensure, maintain, and garner public support.

The rise of indirect costs

The Games are more than just a sporting event and temporary home to a growing number of spectators, media, and athletes, along with their trainers, equipment, and national officials. The Games provide the opportunity, indeed the necessity, for infrastructure provision. As athletes and spectators arrive, they need to be met with new and expanded airport facilities, transport links, and hotel accommodation. The Games provides a tremendous opportunity for all kinds of regional planning objectives and urban makeovers that have long been in in the works and in the imagination of local elites.

Tokyo 1964 was a turning point in the growth of indirect spending. The connection between the government and the construction sector in Japan is so close that the term 'construction state' (*Dokken kokka*) is used with reference to the alliance of politicians, construction firms, and land development companies. Not coincidental that Tokyo's winning bid was led by the construction minister. No surprise then that the hosting of the 1964 Games sparked a massive building program. More than $2.8 billion was spent on the rebuilding of the city's sewage system, 100 km. of superhighways, two new subway lines, a refurbishing of the port and airport, a monorail, new hotels, and a bullet train from Tokyo to Osaka. The Tokyo Games provided the platform for a major makeover of the city.

These indirect costs now constitute a significant element in the overall cost of hosting the Games. Table 5.2 compares the direct costs of operations and provision of sporting venues with the indirect costs of infrastructure. This table is best used as a very rough guide. I have pulled together this comparative data from a variety of different sources and its main use is as a general guide rather than as precise metric. There is a variety of reporting errors and underestimated lack of transparency that makes assessing Olympic costs more like a guesstimation than an estimation. While these figures may be more hazy than precise, the overall trend is clear. There are a lot of indirect costs to hosting the Olympic Games.

Table 5.2 Direct and indirect costs of hosting the Olympic Games

Games	Direct costs	Indirect costs
2016 Rio	4.5	11.6
2014 Sochi	21.8	36.0
2012 London	10.4	4.6
2000 Vancouver	1.7	4.7
2008 Beijing	6.8	37.1
2006 Turin	4.3	2.7
2004 Athens	2.9	13.0
2002 Salt Lake	2.5	1.2
2000 Sydney	5.0	3.6

All figures are in US2014$ billions.
Source: Calculated by author

There is a trajectory of a steady increase in indirect costs. The era from 1896 to 1904 was the time of limited urban impacts when the Games consisted of small-scale events with little new urban infrastructure. From 1908 to 1932, the Games had gradually increasing impacts, still small-scale, but with some new infrastructure. The 68,000-seat White City stadium was the only venue built for the 1908 Games in London, but stood until 1985, an early example of the long-term urban legacies of hosting the Games. The period from 1936 to 1980 is marked by the construction of large-scale, purpose-built stadia, as well as increasing amounts of infrastructural improvement. This period opens with the global spectacle of Berlin in 1936 and a high point is the mountain of concrete poured for the Tokyo 1964 Games. Since 1980, hosting the Games involves a massive urban transformation, including the provision of venues, the refurbishment of exiting venues, and major infrastructural investment.

The Winter Games can also be described as a trajectory of mounting indirect costs. The first stage from 1924 to 1932 involved very little infrastructural investment. There were few athletes and not much public interest. Fewer than 500 athletes competed in each of the first three Winter Games held in in 1924, 1928, and 1932. In the second stage, from 1936 to 1960, there was a growth in participation and more athletes and visitors necessitated some Olympics-related infrastructure. Squaw Valley in 1960, an event promoted by a local real estate developer, saw the construction of the largest Olympic Village to date. From 1964 onward, the Winter Games saw an increasing number of athletes and a shift toward larger host centers. Small isolated villages could no longer host the Winter Games. And if they did, they had to be transformed and regionally connected. Attention shifted to using the Games as part of regional development strategies. Almost 20 percent of the total costs of the Grenoble Games in France was spent on road construction linking the city to other cities in the wider region. For Sapporo, in 1972, transport investment included extensions to two motorways and construction of a mass transit system.

More-recent Winter Games involve similar large-scale transformations. The Winter Games are now hosted in larger population centers and are used to implement large-scale infrastructure and urban renewal projects. Calgary and Lillehammer in 1988 and 1994, respectively, were not only sporting events but also attempts to stimulate regional and urban economies. The 2002 Winter Games, for example, involved downtown development in Salt Lake City, the construction of seven permanent venues at the winter sports site in Park City, the reconstruction of two interstate routes, and two new light rail systems. The Turin Games were part of attempt to resuscitate an ailing city economy as it shifted from industrial to postindustrial. The Vancouver Games involved a rapid transit link between the airport and the city and an upgrade to the highway between Vancouver and Whistler.

Figure 5.2 Indirect costs: Electric rail in Sochi, Russia, built for the 2014 Winter Games that cost close to US$55 billion

Source: https://upload.wikimedia.org/wikipedia/commons/a/a9/Электропоезд_%22Ласточка%22.JPG

The most expensive Winter Games took place in Sochi Russia in 2014 as winter sport facilities were built from scratch (Figure 5.2). Eleven brand new facilities were built and 20,000 new hotel rooms. Seven new power stations had to be constructed to meet the demand for energy.

Other indirect costs

Although more difficult to quantify as easily as infrastructure, there are also other indirect costs to hosting the Games. Two of the most significant are the social and environmental costs.

Social costs

There are many social costs to hosting the Games. The noise and congestion during the construction phase exacts a toll. I remember visiting Sydney during the lead up to the 2000 Games, and the city felt like a permanent and noisy construction site. There was a standing joke at the time. "What is the difference between Sydney and Belgrade [then in the middle of a war]?' The answer: "One is under constant duress, suffers from loud and incessant noise, and its citizens feel under attack and assaulted. The other is the capital of the former Yugoslavia."

There are also restrictions on civil liberties leading up to and during the period of the Games. Citizens of host cities have limitations placed on their freedom to move and assemble as the Olympic City becomes the securitized city of the constant panopticon.

Host cities have to ensure safety and security. But limitations are placed on the right to assembly and even the right to advertise. In order to maintain their media monopoly, the IOC is always on the lookout for guerilla or ambush marketing, when advertisers seek to get a free ride from the massive exposure afforded by the Games. It is not permitted to walk into an Olympic stadium wearing a Nike shirt or a hat with a logo of a corporation that is not an IOC sponsor. You are not permitted to show a non-IOC-sponsored corporate logo from your place of residency if it is in the media gaze. There is also the temporary privatization and securitization of public spaces. Your city becomes the city of the IOC.

The Games infringes on civil liberties in numerous other ways. Hosting the Games allows local and national authorities to criminalize poverty and homelessness as the 'marginal' are swept up and removed from public view, like so much street rubbish, before the foreign visitors come. In the more authoritarian countries, critics of the regime are often rounded up, as was the case of Beijing 2008. In the lead-up to the World Cup and Olympics, Rio police undertook a 'pacification' of the favelas, aimed at the young and poor of the city's slums.

In the year immediately before the Sydney Olympics, new laws were introduced to prohibit the selling of goods on the street. The homeless population was under greater surveillance in public space and one 1999 regulation gave the local police power to limit access to public spaces used for Olympic events. The state and federal government granted emergency police powers in the name of Olympics security. Various forms of legislation were introduced before the Vancouver Games that gave authorities the power to place the homeless in temporary shelters, and there was increased CCTV surveillance.

Hosting the Games involves an increased securitization of a city. Now while this comes with some benefits to public safety, there are also costs and longer legacies. There is a militarization and securitization of the host city. All in the name of security and a 'self-conscious semiotics of security.'[3] The Olympics securitization of the city involves more perimeter security, stockaded venues, privatized/securitized spaces, surveillance regimes, and fortress urbanism. Sochi became a fortress under military control rather than an open city, welcoming the world.

There are also the social costs involved in the construction of the Games. Construction workers are often pressed to work in difficult and dangerous conditions as the deadline for the opening ceremonies approaches. Migrant workers from Eastern Europe were employed on contract to build the facilities for the Sochi Games. Human Rights Watch reported hundreds of deaths of construction workers and pervasive nonpayment of ways. At least $8 million in back wages has not been paid.

There are also the displacements caused by the construction of venues and infrastructure. More than 700,000 people were evicted to make way for the 1988 Seoul Games. More than 15,000 people were evicted from public housing projects that were demolished for Olympic venues for the 1996 Games in Atlanta.

According to the Center on Housing Rights and Evictions more than 2 million people were displaced due to Olympics-related projects from 1992 to 2012.[4] Some 77,200 were evicted in Rio to make way for the 2016 Olympics. The most dramatic case of displacement was the Beijing Games, where it is estimated that 1.5 million were displaced. The Chinese government claims that only 15,000 were displaced because they only include those impacted by venue construction, whereas the higher figure includes those displaced by the related infrastructure projects. To some extent, much of the infrastructure would have occurred over time even without the Games. Displacement was and remains a feature of China's rapid urban growth. But the 2008 Games justified, accelerated, and reinforced displacement trends already apparent in the breakneck development of China's capital.

The increase in rents, gentrification, and the replacement of cheaper with more-expensive housing, all part of the Olympic experience, leads to direct and indirect displacement. The Games reinforce rather than undermine regressive social outcomes. So while not the cause, they are definitely not the solution.

The Games tend to have regressive impact on the housing market, negatively affecting the poorest and the more vulnerable. When we think of costs and benefits, we must also ask who pays and who gains? It is difficult to escape the conclusion that the social costs of hosting the Games are imposed most heavily on the poor, while the benefits accrue to the richest. The Olympic Games is one of the most regressive megaprojects on the planet.

Environmental costs

Beijing will host the 2022 Winter Olympics. Where will the snow come from for a winter event in a city and region that has little snow? Beijing sits on a plain so the events needing altitude, such as skiing and snowboarding, will be held between 55 and 100 miles away, with some of them being held on the edge of the Gobi Desert: winter events in a dry desert where snowfall rarely exceeds 10 inches. The snow for the Beijing Winter Olympic Games, like much of the snow for the Sochi Games, will come from water drawn from lakes and streams, super-cooled into ice crystals and then shot from a cannon. The environmental impacts in a region subject to desertification could be profound and long lasting.

The choice of Beijing to host the Winter Games highlights the environmental impacts of the Games.

Few worried or cared about the environment consequences of the early Games of the modern period. They were of limited size and had minimal environmental consequences. Then the 'building big' era was inaugurated with the 1936 Games in Berlin when the Nazis exploited the propaganda opportunity. After the austerity of the immediate post-WWII era, Berlin became the role model as the Games became a gargantuan spectacle: building new and building big often on greenfield sites. The Games were the perfect opportunity to achieve the modernist dream of rewriting urban landscapes and transforming local environments. The only constraint was money, not an environmental sensitivity.

The first environmental change was brought about by the massive cost overruns of Montreal in 1976. The LA Games of 1984 marked a shift from this new build model to a mixture of new build and reuse of existing facilities. This had an environmental impact but was the result of cost-cutting rather than pursuing environmental goals. The more-explicit use of environmental goals slowly emerged in the 1990s. For the 1992 Games, Barcelona built a new waterfront and upgraded an abandoned industrial railway site as well as making numerous improvements throughout the metro area, including new roads, a new sewer system, and the creation or improvement of more than 200 parks, plazas, and streets. There was a conscious greening of the city.

Environmental protection and sustainability was an integral part of the 1994 Winter Games in Lillehammer. Norway's then-prime minister, Gro Harlem Brundtland, was the chair of a 1987 UN Commission that promoted the idea and practice of sustainable development. In 1996, the Olympic Charter was amended to address the issue of sustainable development, and the environment became the third pillar of the movement, beside sport and culture.

Cities now have to address issues of sustainability in their bid documents. But this is more rhetorical than practical, a form of legitimation in a more environmentally conscious age rather than a practical guide. Part of the problem lies in the difficulty of assessing carbon and ecological and water footprints. There are few agreed-upon data sources or standard techniques.

It is a remarkable and disturbing fact that we have no formal agreed-upon criteria for assessing the environmental impact of the Games. One of the biggest mega-events in the world goes ahead with no defined rules for measuring or monitoring its environmental impact. There is also no real follow-up to a host city's claim to sustainability.

Despite a lack of formal monitoring by the IOC, there was a shift as some cities took the opportunity to promote a greener development. The main site of the Sydney Games of 2000 was built on Homebush Bay, an inner-ring contaminated site. Athens undertook large-scale public investments in water supply and mass transit. The Games in Turin 2006 sought to reduce carbon footprints, minimize water use in snow making, promote eco-friendly hotels, and introduce carbon offsets. For the 2008 Games, Beijing replaced its 18,000-bus fleet with more fuel-efficient and less-polluting vehicles.

The 2012 London Games were promoted as a green Games with greater use of renewable energy and water recycling. The lower Lea Valley was remediated. Only wood from sustainable sources was used and the soil removed for the swimming pools was used in the landscaping of local parks. Even with these projects, the Games generated around 3.45 million tons of CO_2.

There has been shift in the Games toward carbon offsetting in the transport of visiting athletes and spectators, greater use of renewable energy, and reducing the impacts of construction and maintenance.

But we have no solid basis to answer the basic question of what are the environmental costs and benefits of hosting the Olympics. An honest answer has proved elusive, as analyses are hampered by lack of proper accounting methods, technical issues, and the lack of available data. Organizations seeking to promote, justify, or attract the Games generate the vast majority of analyses. While these studies highlight the positive benefits, fewer studies examine the costs of the Games. And the environmental turn is not a continuous line of progress. For every London, there is also a Sochi.

Sochi is the worst case of high environmental costs despite a bid that promised a green environmental Games. The 2014 Sochi Games were an environmental disaster. A zero-waste pledge was quickly breached. There was illegal dumping of construction waste. A limestone quarry was turned into a construction waste site that will contaminate local water for the next 10 to 15 year. More than 8,000 acres of Sochi National Park were cleared to build Olympics facilities. The Olympic Village was built on a World Heritage Site and rare wetlands and other important habitats were destroyed.[5]

We are entering a new era in which popular support for the Games is undermined by the unease over the rising costs and environment impacts. An environmentally friendly Games is likely to be a more expensive Games. But hosting a cheaper but environmentally damaging Games is also

unacceptable. Rising costs and greater scrutiny of environmental consequences and impact may make hosting the Games a less-attractive proposition and tougher sell. With fewer bid cities, the IOC becomes more reliant
on regressive regimes and host cities where the environmental requirements
may be part of the bid but not the reality on the ground. In this scenario, even
a gold medal will lose its luster.

An environmental rhetoric is now institutionalized within the IOC. The
changing of the charter and new bid requirements, as well as the constant
mentioning in IOC documentation of an environmental sensitivity, all suggest a greater environmental awareness and sensitivity. But while the bidding and hosting of the Games has led to greater environmental awareness
in the host countries, little progress, apart from London in 2012, has been
made in reducing the carbon footprint of the Games, or in an honest environmental impact assessment of the Games.

Notes

1 Preuss, H. (2004). *The Economics of Staging the Olympics: A Comparison of the Games, 1972–2008*. Cheltenham: Edward Elgar Publishing.
2 Flyvberg, B. and Stewart, A. (2012) *Olympic Proportions: Cost and Cost Over-run and the Olympics 1960–2012*. Said Business School Working Paper. Univer-sity of Oxford. http://eureka.sbs.ox.ac.uk/4943/1/SSRN-id2382612_(2).pdf
3 Boyle, P. and Haggerty, K. D. (2009) Spectacular security: Mega-events and the sector complex. *International Political Sociology* 3: 257–274.
4 Centre on Housing Rights and Evictions (2007) *Fair Play for Housing Rights: Megaevents, Olympic Games and Housing Rights*. Geneva: Centre on Housing Rights and Evictions.
    Center of Housing rights and Evictions (2008) *One World, Whose Dream? Housing Rights, Violations and the Beijing Games*. Geneva: Centre on Housing Rights and Evictions.
5 Beans, L. (2014) 4 reasons the Sochi Olympics are an environmental disaster. *Ecowatch*. www.ecowatch.com/4-reasons-the-sochi-olympics-are-an-environmental-disaster-1881859802.html

6 Costs and benefits

If truth be told, objective cost-benefit analysis of hosting the Games remains at a rudimentary stage, with few accurate or comprehensive studies and little comparative data. Much of the massive public investment in the Olympic Games often goes unrecorded. The analyses by consultancy groups employed by bid committees are deeply flawed by wildly optimistic assessment of benefits and a severe underestimation of costs. The OCOG budget, for example, does not include permanent venue construction. Most academic studies, in contrast, suggest that the benefits do not outweigh the costs.[1]

Let us start with simple question: do the Games make money or lose money? The most optimistic analysis is by the sports economist Holger Preuss.[2] In a detailed analysis of comparing selected direct costs and revenues for Summer Games held between 1972 and 2008, Preuss found that, at least since 1972 and especially since 1984, hosting the Games has meant improved infrastructure, increased income and employment in the city, a raising of the profile of the city, and the possibility of increased tourism and foreign investment. The Games tend to accelerate development projects long in the pipeline.

Preuss found that ever since Montreal in 1976, most OCOGs ended with a slight surplus. A word of warning. He only included the direct costs on Olympic projects, ignored the indirect infrastructural investments, and relied on official reports, which have a high degree of inaccuracy, and, for Games held between 2004 and 2008, he used the official estimates rather than actual costs. Using this data, he found that hosting the Games need not be a giant money loser, if direct investments in sports venues are kept under control and the indirect costs of infrastructure provision are offloaded. He identifies four scenarios: A *worst case*, as with Montreal 1976, where a city directly finances the infrastructure. The Olympics boost soon fades and the city is left with a huge debt. A *neutral case*, as with Los Angeles in 1984, where there is little direct and indirect investment and so the Olympics boost in such things as increased tourism leads to net positive effects. A *most likely case,* where new infrastructure is required but is paid for by the city or the government. The longer-term positive impacts may outweigh the debt repayments borne by the taxpayers. The *best case* is where the indirect investments in infrastructure are financed by public or public/private ventures and hosting leads to no debt and long-term positive effects on the global image and economic competitiveness of the city. While Preuss provides example of the first three – the *most likely* for example includes Munich, Barcelona, Sydney, and Athens – he provides no example of the *best case.* Like the fabled unicorn, it may be more the product of a fertile imagination than an actual reality.

Preuss suggests a positive economic legacy from hosting the Games of a small financial surplus, structural improvements to the city, including new and improved sports facilities, and an enhanced international image. However, each of Preuss's conclusions is subject to some scrutiny. The financial surplus conclusion, for example, often refers to the surplus in the revenues that the local organizing committee generates over what they expend in operating and infrastructure investment. It often ignores or downplays the massive public investment in the hosting of the Games. The Atlanta Games, for example, reported a small surplus, yet this ignores the approximately $2 billion spent by public authorities, including $996 million of federal government investment, $226 million in state funds, and $857 million in local funds. The costs are borne by public authorities, while the revenues are privatized by private or nonprofit organizations that are neither democratically elected nor publicly accountable.

But even this most optimistic analysis comes with some caveats. It does not, for example, consider the distribution of costs and benefits, who wins and who loses? Most studies find that the economic impact of the Games is regressive, with most of the costs borne locally, especially by the more-marginal urban residents displaced to make way for the Games, while most of the benefits accrue to local elites and a global media market. There is a profound social dimension to the distribution of costs and benefits.

The big winners of any Olympic windfall are the political regimes and economic elites running the city that have the opportunity to reshape the city's desired image and make a great deal of money in the process.

The very biggest winners are, of course, the construction and land development companies, who do very well from the contracts associated with the direct investment in sports venues and athlete accommodation and from the river of indirect investments of infrastructural provision. Large and politically connected real estate and construction companies benefit most from the Games.

The city's general population also may benefit through increased spending and employment especially during the construction period of the Games. There even may be a slight multiplier effect, as the Games can act as a Keynesian pump primer of the local urban economy. The short-term economic impact varies according to when the Games are held. Games-related expenditure made during a recession have a more positive effect, increasing aggregate demand during a downturn than those made in economic recoveries and booms when the expenditures can crowd out other forms of spending and lead to price increases. Infrastructure investments can provide a form of fiscal stimulus to a city with a depressed economy and slack labor market, but in a buoyant economy the extra jobs in construction are more likely to come at the expense of other sectors. It is also likely that the types of cities that decide to mount bids are on an economic upswing and poised for growth, and winning the bid is more likely to stunt rather than accelerate growth.

The losers are always the low-income residents of city. Hosting the Games crowds out other investments, especially redistributional investments in social welfare and education that benefit the less-wealthy while the construction of venues and infrastructure can displace low-income residents, and raise rents and property prices. Most of the negative costs are borne by the weaker groups in the city, especially those inhabiting city sites designated for redevelopment. Preparations for the Games often involves the spatial removal of the poor and the marginal. Hosting the Games is socially regressive. The Games are a classic example of the privatization of benefits and the socialization of costs. It is the public subsidization of an event whose main benefits are captured by the rich and well-connected.

Costs and benefits

We need to ask another question: are the total costs outweighed by the aggregate benefits?

We should not look to the official reports or the many reports paid for by business promoters of the Games and local OCOGs. These official and semi-official cost-benefit analyses, especially done in the lead up to the bid, have the rosiest assumptions of future benefits, downplay the costs, treat costs as benefits, ignore opportunity costs, and use multipliers that are way too large. For example, building or refurbishing an athletic venue in these supportive analyses is always treated as a benefit, whereas it can turn into a cost. The main central site of the 2004 Athens Games is falling into disrepair, an empty shell that costs money even as it sits idle and unproductive (Figure 6.1). Venues underused and rarely used after the Games can quickly

Figure 6.1 The main athletic stadium used for the 2004 Athens Games. It now lies idle most of the time

Source: John Rennie Short

devalorize, turning what were once projected as future benefits into fiscal burdens. Studies that compare 'before and after' found that cost-benefit analyses before the Games always promised increased tourism and additional employment, whereas analyses after the Games found that the one-time event had no lasting impact on business activity or city employment.[3]

Most sponsored studies and official OCOG reports ignore opportunity costs, such as building hospitals, financing education, or even just letting taxpayers keep their money. Nagano had debts that amounted to $20,000 for each and every city household after hosting the 1998 Winter Games. There is a consistent pattern in the official studies that promote the Games: the initial costs are underestimated; some costs are treated as benefits, while all benefits are exaggerated; and public subsidies are discounted or ignored. Even when Games will actually lose money, organizers will always claim a net positive benefit.

For more critical and independent assessments, we need to look at the academic literature and here very few independent studies find a positive economic impact.

In one of the most comprehensive analysis, economists Robert Baade and Victor Matheson looked at costs and benefits associated with Olympic Games, both Summer and Winter, from 1972 to 2002.[4] On the cost side, they included three major categories: general infrastructure, such as transportation; specific sports infrastructure required for competition venues; and operational costs, including general administration, the opening and closing ceremony, and security. They identified three major categories of benefits: the short-run benefits of tourist spending during the Games; the long-run benefits or the 'Olympic legacy,' which might include improvements in infrastructure and increased trade, foreign investment, or tourism after the Games; and intangible benefits, such as the 'feel-good effect' or civic pride. Their overwhelming conclusion is that the Olympics are a money-losing proposition for host cities, resulting in positive net benefits only under very specific and unusual circumstances, Barcelona being the best-known example. Furthermore, the cost-benefit imbalance is worse for cities in the global South compared to cities in the global North. Their overall conclusion, "the long run benefits of hosting the Games prove to be elusive."[5]

Andrew Zimbalist pulled together a large body of work on the economic impacts of hosting sport mega-events, the World Cup as well as the Olympic Games. His overall conclusion is similar, "the promised benefits are not forthcoming."[6]

In terms of short-run impacts, most studies find little effect on real GDP, employment, tourism, taxable sales, hotel occupancy, or airport usage. There are also short-terms costs of disruption to business and households during the construction and hosting of the Games. Moreover, the more-recent Games hosted in an era more sensitive to security issue can leave a legacy of greater surveillance and police control of public space.

Long-run economic impacts include tourism and trade/investment. Few studies find a large positive impact on either. There are also long-term costs, such as debt repayments with high opportunity costs. Vancouver has to service a $1 billion debt from the Winter Games that cannot be spent on education, health care, or arts financing.

Let us look at some of the 'benefits' in more detail.

Tourism

In the short term, while some new tourists may be attracted to a host city, others are put off by the costs and the crowds. Beijing saw fewer international visitors during the month they were hosting the Olympics in 2008 compared to the same month in previous years, and Utah ski resorts noticed a dip in traffic during the 2001–02 ski season that coincided with the Salt Lake City Games.[7]

Tourism is depressed during the Games as regular tourists avoid the Olympics crush. The UK received 5 percent fewer foreign visitors in August 2012 than in August 2011. Theatres and museums in London reported 20 percent fewer patrons in the August of the Olympics compared to the previous August.[8]

Hosting the Games produces displacement effects, with some tourists turned away by the crowds and the traffic in host cities. The relatively low ticket sales in many Games suggests that the Olympics are becoming more of a global media event, rather than a real-time, real-place event attended physically by visitors.

For tourism over the longer term, the pattern is mixed.[9] Promoters of the Sydney Olympics estimated that tourism would quadruple after the 2000 Sydney Games, but there was no uptick. Long-haul tourism, it seems, does not experience a post-Olympics bump. Other host cities, such as Calgary (1988) and Lillehammer (1994), saw limited increases in tourism after their Games. After hosting the 1994 Winter Olympics, the Norwegian national and local authorities expected a 'big boom' in tourism; the actual effects were much less, and 40 percent of the full-service hotels in Lillehammer-went bankrupt after the Games. A few cities have turned the Games into a platform for increased tourism in the longer term. Barcelona in 1992 used the games to emerge as a major international tourist attraction, and the Utah ski economy saw a boost in the years after the 2002 Salt Lake City Games (Figure 6.2).

Figure 6.2 Improved winter sports facilities for the 2002 Salt Lake City Games did lead to increased tourism in the area

Source: John Rennie Short

Economic impacts

Does hosting an Olympiad improve a city's economic position? The answer: Most studies find that while there may be a temporary decline in unemployment, there are few long-term benefits.[10]

Two authors matched Olympics host cities with bid cities that were finalists for the Olympic Games, but were not selected. Looking at post-Olympics impacts on real gross domestic product per capita and trade openness between 1950 and 2005, they found no long-term positive impacts of hosting an Olympics.[11]

This finding was confirmed in analyses of exports. One study found that countries hosting the Olympics saw a 20 percent increase in export trade in the years after hosting, relative to similarly situated countries. But they found similar gains for cities that unsuccessfully bid for the Olympics. While hosting the Games can increase exports, the same effect is found for cities that bid but did not win. In effect, cities that bid for the games signal openness to trade and investments. It is not necessary to win the bid – the bid itself sends a message to investors that the city is open for international business. Hosting the Games provide no more benefits than does simply bidding.[12]

It is better to bid and not win than bid and win. You get the same effect without the billions in investment. Bidding but not winning the Games may be the best strategy to leverage footloose capital and make a global splash. The worst strategy may be to both bid and win, and then have to make all those investments that may never pay off.

Even at the more granular level of city case studies, the lack of positive impacts is confirmed. One study of the 2002 Winter Games in Salt Lake City looked at taxable sales in the counties in which Olympic events took place and found that some sectors, such as hotels and restaurants, prospered while other retailers, such as general merchandisers and department stores, suffered. Overall, the gains in the hospitality industry were lower than the losses experienced by other sectors in the economy.[13]

A caution: Cost-benefit analysis has the trapping of science but is, in fact, an art. What counts as cost or benefit is a vital decision that influences the results. How do you estimate the costs and benefits, and in what time frame, with what valuations? These are social and political questions, rather than narrowly econometric ones. So, cost-benefit analysis is more imperfect and judgmental than precise and neutral. The interpretive range is clear in the lively debate that occurred over the employment impact of the 1996 Atlanta Games. One study found significant positive effects of the 1996 Atlanta Games. The authors noted an increase in employment of 293,000 jobs, a 17 percent boost in the counties of Georgia close to Olympics activity. A subsequent paper disputed these findings and found only short-term effects concentrated in the sectors of retail trade, accommodation and food services, and arts, entertainment, and recreation. A rebuttal to the rebuttal found a statistically significant post-Olympics employment gains in counties affected by the Olympics that exceeded employment gains in the rest of the counties in Georgia by 11 percent by the end of 2000.[14]

With the passage of time, it is becomes easier to evaluate the longer-term effects of hosting the Games. A 2008 study of the 1972 Munich Games, able to take a longer-term perspective, found that income in Olympics regions grew significantly faster than in other German regions but, in contrast, no employment effects were identified.[15]

Sophisticated statistics analysis can also uncover what would have been the impact if a city had not hosted the Games. A no-Sydney Olympics counterfactual comparing data from 1997/1998 to 2005/2006 found that hosting the 2000 Games reduced household consumption in Australia by $2.1 billion. In other words, hosting the 2000 Summer Olympics cost Australia a significant decrease in consumption and corresponding suppression of economic growth.[16]

In summary, most objective studies find few positive economic impacts of hosting the Games. Even hard-headed investment advisors conclude that the Games provide few benefits, are based on faulty projections and caution that they are not a good opportunity for investors.[17]

While individual case studies may need some careful consideration, the overall conclusion from the mass of independent studies makes it clear that costs often outweigh benefits, benefits are slight, and official estimates are not to be trusted. The overwhelming conclusion of independent studies: the measurable benefits of the Game are slight or non-existent, over both short and long term, while the costs are real and substantial.

There are some success stories. Los Angeles 1984 was done on the cheap with no new building or infrastructure provision, and so the OCOG made a profit and there was an uptick in tourism. The 1992 Games was part of the revival of Barcelona in post-Franco Spain and helped the city to gain international recognition that subsequently increased tourism.

The success stories of Los Angeles and Barcelona are special cases: with little direct or indirect investment for Los Angeles, while in Barcelona the Games were dovetailed into an emerging plan for the city that was already in the planning stage after being starved of investment for decades under a dictatorship that favored Castilian Madrid over Catalan Barcelona. There were other special factors at work to make the 1992 Games such a success. Almost two-thirds of the cost of the Games came from private sources, and 83 percent of the investment went into improving the city after almost two decades of sluggish growth. The city was primed for stimulus spending. Barcelona, as the capital of Catalonia, was long ignored by the Madrid-based government. The city was a hidden jewel that the Games allowed to sparkle. Spain's entry into the EU also helped the dramatic post-Games uptick in tourism.

But Barcelonas are few and far between in the hosting of the Games. At the other extreme is Sochi, host of the 2014 Winter Games. The estimated cost of the Games, including direct and indirect costs, was around $55 billion. Hosting the Games had two objectives: a regional development project to make Sochi a world-class ski resort, and to reposition a new, more-confident Russia. Posters filled the city with the motto "Russia – Great, New, Open."

There were significant cost overruns because the fixed deadlines enabled construction companies to profit. There was substantial graft and corruption and little oversight, and while some of the expenditures would have occurred as part of regional development polices, the hosting of the Games increased the cost of infrastructure provision.[18] Debt repayments are now considerable and vastly outweigh any benefits from the provision of facilities. While there is an uptick in internal tourism, the event did not generate the predicted foreign tourism. Russia's invasion of Crimea stifled Black Sea tourism from overseas. There is little legacy from the Games, as many venues lie empty or closed. In exchange for years of disruptions, residents get improved transport to the mountain and a more-reliable power supply. Sochi did become a year-round resort, although off-season hotel occupancy rates are only around 60 percent of the summer's almost 100 percent rate. As one study reports,

> The main legacy of the Games is oversized infrastructure at inflated prices paid for almost exclusively by the public. . . . As if the $55 billion of total costs were not enough, the government will have to subsidize the operation and maintenance of venues, tourist and transport infrastructure in the order of $1.2 billion per year for the foreseeable future.[19]

So why bid?

The economic costs of hosting the Olympics far outpace the benefits. So why do cities bother to bid at all? Three reasons. The first is that while the Games may provide few net benefits, they do always benefit someone. The economic and political elites of a city benefit most and so they want to host the Games, privatize the benefits, and offload the cost to the public. The Games provide an opportunity to make private profit at public expense.

A second reason is that elites want to reposition their city in an increasingly competitive global economy. As the world flattens through globalization and the easier flow of capital, people, and goods, cities are competing for mobile capital and fickle tourists. Behind the hard-headed plans are the dreams of creating a global city. The Games provide the metanarrative for the creation of the global city, well connected to the outside world, presenting a positive image to potential visitors, tourists and investors. The positive image is one of modernity and multiculturalism, part of a shared global discourse while also adding a touch of the uniquely local: a distinctive place connected to a shared global space: a city with global connections and local distinctiveness. Hosting the Games provides the platform for making a global city.

Finally, there is the feel-good effect. In order to understand Olympics bids, it is better to be an anthropologist than an economist. Because even without the naked self-interest, there are other forces at work. In cities that host the Games and in the immediate aftermath, there is often a profound sense of community, an uptick in volunteerism, and a general sense of well-being. The glow does not warm everyone but many city residents, in survey after survey, report positive feelings about their city and their community immediately after a successful hosting of the Games. This is difficult to estimate. Difficult, but not impossible. One survey found that people across the United Kingdom collectively valued the opportunity to host the Olympics at about £2 billion, still well short of the close to £16 billion cost of hosting. In other words, people overpaid for the feel-good affect. Like most Olympic costs, there was a substantial overrun. While people in London were willing to pay £22 per year for 10 years, people in Glasgow were, on average, only willing to pay £11. The national event reinforced regional inequalities in the UK.[20]

Naked self-interest, civic pride, and the desire to affirm a city's status as a "world city" are all reasons for bidding and hosting the Games. But the disturbing conclusion is that many of the benefits are obtained without hosting the Games. There are few economic enterprises where lack of success has similar outcomes. It would be like getting the flood control benefits without building the dam. The obvious conclusion: Do not build the dam. And do not host the Olympics.

Notes

1 Baade, R. A. and Matheson, V. A. (2016). Going for the gold: The economics of the Olympics. *The Journal of Economic Perspectives* 30: 201–218.
   Porter, P. K. and Fletcher, D. (2008) The economic impact of the Olympic Games: *Ex ante* predictions and *ex poste* reality. *Journal of Sport Management* 22: 470–486.
   Zimbalist, A. (2016, 2nd ed.) *Circus Maximus: The Economic Gamble Behind Hosting the Olympics and the World Cup*. Washington, DC: Brookings Institution Press.
2 Preuss, H. (2004) *The Economics of Staging the Olympics*. Cheltenham: Edward Elgar.
3 Kasimati, E. (2003) Economic aspects and the Summer Olympics: A review of related research. *International Journal of Tourism Research* 5: 433–444.
   Kirkup, N. and Major, B. (2006) Doctoral foundation paper: The reliability of economic impact studies of the Olympic Games: A post-games study of Sydney 2000 and considerations for London 2012. *Journal of Sport & Tourism* 11: 275–296.
   Porter, P. K. and Fletcher, D. (2008) The economic impact of the Olympic Games: *Ex ante* predictions and *ex poste* reality. *Journal of Sport Management* 22: 470.
4 Baade, R. A. and Matheson, V. A. (2016) Going for the gold: The economics of the Olympics. *Journal of Economic Perspectives* 30: 201–218.
5 Baade and Matheson, *op cit.*, p. 213.
6 Zimbalist, A. (2016, 2nd ed.) *Circus Maximus: The Economic Gamble Behind Hosting the Olympics and World Cup*. Washington, DC: Brookings Institution Press. Quote, p. 5.
7 Dyer, G. (2009) Beijing Olympics fails to boost tourism, figures show. *The Financial Times*. www.ft.com/content/6a0fd5ae-dd77-11dd-930e-000077b07658
8 Ainsworth-Wells, M. (2013) London's Olympic legacy: The results are in. *The Telegraph*. www.telegraph.co.uk/travel/destinations/europe/united-kingdom/england/london/articles/Londons-Olympic-legacy-the-results-are-in/
   Liu, D. and Wilson, R. (2014) The negative impacts of hosting mega-sporting events and intention to travel: A test of the crowding-out effect using the London 2012 Games as an example. *International Journal of Sports Marketing and Sponsorship* 15: 12–26.

9 Fourie, J. and Santana-Gallego, M. (2011) The impact of mega-sport events on tourist arrivals. *Tourism Management* 32: 1364–1370.
10 Tien, C., Lo, H. C., and Lin, H. W. (2011) The economic benefits of mega events: A myth or a reality? A longitudinal study on the Olympic Games. *Journal of Sport Management* 25: 11–23.
11 Billings, S. B. and Holladay, J. S. (2012) Should cities go for the gold? The long-term impacts of hosting the Olympics. *Economic Inquiry* 50(3): 754–772.
12 Rose, A. K. and Spiegel, M. M. (2011) The Olympic effect. *Economic Journal* 121: 652–677.

   Maennig, W. and Richter, F. (2012). Exports and Olympic Games: Is there a signal effect? *Journal of Sports Economics* 13(6): 635–641.
13 Baade, R. A., Baumann, R., and Matheson, V. (2008) Slippery slope? Assessing the economic impact of the 2002 Winter Olympic Games in Salt Lake City. *Utah Economics Department Working Papers*. Paper 45. https://crossworks. holycross.edu/econ_working_papers/45
14 Hotchkiss, J. L., Moore, R. E., and Zobay, S. M. (2003) Impact of the 1996 Summer Olympic Games on employment and wages in Georgia. *Southern Economic Journal*, 691–704.

   Feddersen, A. and Maennig, W. (2013) Employment effects of the Olympic Games in Atlanta 1996 reconsidered. *International Journal of Sport Finance* 8: 95–111.

   Hotchkiss, J. L., Moore, R. E., and Rios-Avila, F. (2015). Reevaluation of the employment impact of the 1996 Summer Olympic Games. *Southern Economic Journal* 81: 619–632.
15 Jasmand, S. and Maennig, W. (2008) Regional income and employment effects of the 1972 Munich Summer Olympic Games. *Regional Studies* 42: 991–1002.
16 Giesecke, J. A. and Madden, J. R. (2011) Modelling the economic impacts of the Sydney Olympics in retrospect – Game over for the bonanza story? *Economic Papers: A Journal of Applied Economics and Policy* 30(2): 218–232. doi:10.1111/j.1759-3441.2011.00109.x
17 Von Rekowsky, R. (2013) Are the Olympics a gold opportunity for investors? *Fideilty Investments: Investment Insights*. www.fidelity.com/bin-public/060_ www_fidelity_com/documents/Are%20the%20Olympics%20a%20Golden%20 Opportunity%20for%20Investors_Fidelity.pdf
18 Forrest, B. (2014) Putin's run for gold. *Vanity Fair*. www.vanityfair.com/news/ politics/2014/02/sochi-olympics-russia-corruption

   Vasilyeva, N. (2015) Oligarchs unload Sochi Olympic assets to recoup investment. *The Morning Call*. www.mcall.com/sports/olympics/mc-olympics-russia-sochi-costly-legacy-20150207-story.html#page=1
19 Muller, M. (2014) After Sochi: Costs and benefits of Russia's Olympic Games. *Eurasian Geography and Economics* 55: 628–655.
20 Atkinson, G., Mourato, S., Szymanski, S., and Ozdemiroglu, E. (2008) Are we willing to pay enough to back the bid?: Valuing the intangible impacts of London's bid to host the 2012 Summer Olympic Games. *Urban Studies* 45: 419–444.

7   Urban legacies

Legacy – the notion that host cities have something positive to show after the end of the Games – arises late in the discourse of the Olympics movement in scattered documents in the 1980s after the Munich, Montreal, and Moscow Games did little to enhance the image of hosting the Games. At a time of crisis, 'legacy' emerged as a possible face-saver. Just as the glory of hosting the Games was beginning to fade, and the cost and criticisms were beginning to rise, so the idea of the Games as leaving a positive legacy was developed as a way to encourage and legitimize bids. Legacy provides the cover for escalating costs and is a carrot for potential bid cities. It is invoked by the IOC because it creates more bids and, thus, strengthens their bargaining hand in their franchise model.[1]

The IOC is adept at coopting popular ideas into the Olympics message. During the Cold War, the Games were promoted as a stage for international understanding. As the Cold War ended and the costs of hosting the Games escalated, the IOC incorporated the contemporary issues of environmental awareness and sustainability. In 1999, the IOC formally introduced the terms *sustainable development* and *legacy* into its charter to counter and respond to the criticisms of rising costs and the negative environmental impacts of the Games. The Games were expensive but, so the new legacy argument went, they left a permanent legacy that promised long-term positive impacts for the host city: a new image in an increasingly competitive world, new and improved sporting venues, environmental improvement, urban revitalization, better transportation, and increased economic activity. The IOC on its official website notes, "The Games can be a tremendous catalyst for change in a host city." They list a series of legacies, including sporting legacies, social legacies, environmental legacies, urban legacies, and economic legacies. All bid cities now have to reply to an IOC questionnaire asking about the long-term impact and the legacy effects of hosting the Games, the Games's place in the long-term planning of the city, the level of public and government support, the existing and planned sporting infrastructure, and the environmental impact of the Games. The IOC provides few solid guidelines and no financing to plan, build, or measure the positive legacy. Legacy, for the IOC, is a justifying rhetoric rather than a prescribed practice. So, we cannot look to the IOC for a good guide, rather we have to look at the experience of host cities. In the remainder of this chapter, I will focus on the more-tangible legacies of a city's reputation, transport networks, venues and sites, and more general urban transformations. I will also raise the much-less-discussed legacy of a more securitized city.

Reputational legacies

Hosting the Olympic Games can change the reputation of city. For citizens and residents of host cities, the Games can improve civic pride, reinforce feelings of community, and generate a positive atmosphere in the city, at least in the lead-up to, and very often during, a successful Games. Even if temporary or fleeting, the sense of community in a host city during the Games is palpable. The festival-like atmosphere, the sense of shared and collective experience promotes a feel-good factor that can paper-over dissent and criticisms of the economic costs and socially regressive nature of the benefits. The investment decisions made by the local elites and the OCOG to host the Games are often forgotten, dismissed, or marginalized during the Games as the city and its residents put their best face forward to a global audience. Later, disillusion may set in when the full costs and failed promises are fully revealed.

The Games can also become an important transformative experience for a city's external reputation. Local elites claim that hosting the Games will improve the global reputation of the city, enhancing international competitiveness and its perception in the wider world.

The Games do allow a city to showcase itself to a global audience and become more globally connected. For two weeks, the city is constantly mentioned and represented in the world's media. New or greatly expanded international airports are standard requirements, as are new road and mass transit linkages from the airport to the rest of the city. Hosting the Games allows the city to achieve global recognition and greater global connectivity, with the possibility of increased tourism and investment. There are some successes. Barcelona successfully used the Games to improve its international image and reposition itself as a major tourist destination, almost doubling the number of foreign visitors two years after the Games compared to two years prior to the Games.[2]

A city that hosts a successful Games can increase its value as an international destination as well as increase and upgrade its stock of athletic venues. A well-run Games can create increased administrative capabilities, new political alliances, and a positive imagery that can then be used to attract subsequent competitions. The city now has greater traction in its bids to host other mega-events. That Seoul hosted the 1988 Games allowed it to successfully compete as one of the sites for the 2002 World Cup. With new facilities, a proven track record of organization, growth coalitions already in place, new infrastructure, and name recognition, an Olympic host city can successfully compete for other mega-events. Hosting the Games can put a city on a new trajectory of global competitiveness, as Olympics success can breed even more success. In Beijing, the Bird's Nest stadium, originally built for the 2008 Games, will be used for the opening and closing ceremonies of the 2022 Winter Games.

Hosting the Games signals the city's reentry or rebranding on the international stage. For Seoul, it marked the opening of the city and the economy to the outside world, and for Barcelona, an international repositioning of the city as a way to escape the political and discursive dominance of Madrid in a post-Franco Spain. The need for global legitimacy prompted the Chinese government to spend billions on the Beijing Games.

While there are many anecdotal claims, there are few empirical studies of reputational shifts. As a rough proxy for changing reputations, we can measure tourist reactions. Research that looked at the impact on the consumer on short-haul tourism found contradictory results. For already well-established cities, the Games did little to change perceptions and subsequent travel. Some were attracted by the hosting of the Games, others, more concerned with culture, were put off after watching the Games. Hosting the Games did not have a large positive impact on changing tourist perceptions.[3]

Even if the Games work out well, the numbers seeing the city in a more positive light are offset by those put off by the crowds, the crush, and the negative imagery and publicity.

For the more positively viewed recent Games, such as London and Vancouver, the long-term impact is slight. These cities already have a positive reputation for many investors and tourists, so it is unlikely that hosting the Games shifts the dial of their global reputation. The Games did, however, raise concerns about displacement and cost overruns; so, the overall impact is small and sometimes negative.

The reputational legacy is problematic because there is also the chance that the host city may end up with a more-negative view. Atlanta, Sochi, and Rio all emerged as much tainted as celebrated. The negative press included cost overruns, the assault on civil rights, displacement, corruption, and deleterious environmental impacts. The cities' dubious record on social justice was exposed by the Games.

The Games do little for cities with a positive reputation but can undermine the reputation of cities struggling to establish a global reputation, especially

Figure 7.1 Legacies: Centennial Park, Atlanta. This park in downtown Atlanta is one of the few positive permanent benefits of the 1996 Games

Source: John Rennie Short

if the Games are not viewed as a resounding success. Beijing highlights the dilemma. While the opening ceremonies, spectacular architecture, and smooth efficiency of the Games helped to improve the global image, the renewed scrutiny highlighted issues of displacement, human rights, and air quality.

We have to conclude that hosting the Games does not improve the reputation of a city viewed positively before the Games. And while it can improve the visibility of less-well-known cities, it comes with the added risk that its new reputation may as likely be negative as positive. Although hosting the Games can leave a small positive reputation, this may lessen over time as criticisms of the Games in general continue to mount. Hosting has the potential to have a negative reputational legacy if the Games exposes economic and social problems that would be less well known without the bright glare of global media coverage.

Transport legacies

In order to host the Olympic Games, cities have to build, improve, and enhance their transport connections. They have to move large numbers of people very quickly from the airport to the city, and around the city and region to the various sites and venues.

Transport improvements are one of the biggest non-sporting legacies. One study that looked at five host cities – Barcelona, Atlanta, Sydney, Athens, and London – found some common legacies: new and improved airport city connections, improvements to the main airport, creation and revitalization of parks that had good transport access, additional road capacity, and more-advanced transport knowledge systems to guide traffic flows.[4] These are important and long-lasting legacies. The experience of individual cities varied. Atlanta paid little attention to public transport, resulting in traffic jams. The 1996 Atlanta Games are considered a transport mess. There was little lasting impact in Sydney.

The more-positive experience of Barcelona, Athens, and London shows that it takes careful planning to devise a system to meet both the temporary peak demand of the Games and to enhance post-Games travel. There is often a mismatch between the transport dreams of the host cities and the urban realities. The more valuable and long-lasting legacies emerge from those cities that successfully balance the short-term transport needs of the Games in the city with the longer-term post-Games urban development needs.[5]

In the case of Athens, often used as a case study for cost overruns and poor post-Games use of venues, there was a more-careful matching of the transport plans for the city of the event and the post-Games city. A new international airport, long on the list of needs of the city, was built. The road network was expanded, including 120 km. of new roads and 40 km. of motorways. One metro line was upgraded and two new metro lines were built. A new toll way (Attiki Odos) built for the Games, continues to connect the airport with the port and connects with the metro and rail systems. One study concluded:

> In summary, many transportation projects were built in Athens due to the Olympics. The catalytic effect allowed Greek authorities to implement long-standing projects designed around improving accessibility and mobility in the Greek capital. Many of these projects have proven to be beneficial for Athenians following the Games. In particular, the airport, the metro and the peripheral highway, Attiki Odos, have enjoyed popularity ever since. . . . The tangible legacies Athens created were tremendous. For example, access to the airport today is provided by private cars and express buses via the Athiki Odos, Metro Line 3 and the suburban rail. Furthermore, the traffic management centre provides essential function to relieve congestion in the inner city.[6]

In the case of Atlanta, Rio, and Sydney, in contrast, the transport for the Games had little longer-term legacy for the city. For a successful transport legacy, the host city must align the short-term needs for the Games with the long-term requirements of the city. Simply meeting the transport requirement of the Games – getting visitors and athletes to and from the airport and around the scattered venues – does not by itself provide much of a transport legacy for the post-Games city.

The quality and extent of the transport legacy has everything to do with transport planning integration by the host city. It has nothing to do with the IOC, which espouses the notion of legacy but does nothing to finance it. The IOC plays almost no role in ensuring legacy. The IOC has its own priorities regarding the efficiency of the Games, which may or may not align with the longer-term transport needs of a host city. In some cases, a city may sacrifice long-term planning goals in order to secure the bid. The IOC is concerned primarily with the smooth running of the Games, not with the long-term future of the host city.

The legacy of venues and sites

Hosting the Olympic Games involves the construction and refurbishment of sporting venues. Some of them are massive structures, some spectacular pieces of architecture, while others are merely functional. Some are built to impress the global television audience as well as the visitors to the city. But what is their long-term legacy?

On the positive side, they add to the stock of athletic facilities in the city that can then be used to provide opportunities for physical exercise for the local population. And the increased and improved legacy of athletic venues can be used to attract other international mega-events, the world championships of individual sports such as the World Cup. The stadium constructed to host Olympic events can become permanent sites used for subsequent events. The Seoul Olympic stadium was a venue for 2002 FIFA World Cup. In Atlanta, the main athletic stadium became the permanent home of the Atlanta Braves baseball team.

However, the nature of the Games, involving large-scale provision of many venues, often at high cost, raises major legacy concerns. Venues are often built to high IOC standards for crowds that may never be seen again. Highly specific venues, such as the kayak slalom, or the very largest venues, especially the massive main stadium, may never see the level of post-Games usage to justify their initial costs. I remember visiting the Olympic swimming pool in Sydney in 2002. The pool where so many world records were broken only two years previously was being rented out occasionally for children's birthday parties.

On the negative side, there are many examples of Olympic white elephants – venues and complexes underused and abandoned, providing few benefits but still generating costs of debt repayment, maintenance, and security. At worst, some host cities are images of Olympics ruin porn. The case of Sarajevo, host to the 1984 Winter Games, is perhaps the saddest. It is a city where many of the Olympics venues are abandoned or vandalized, or have simply collapsed under the weight of neglect and dereliction.[7]

But there are also cases where the ruins are not simply the result of war and military destruction. They include the forlorn Olympic cauldron that sits beside the freeway in Atlanta. In Athens, the beach volleyball site is returning to weed-covered sand, the diving center is drained, and the pool is polluted but still home to sturdy frogs. The Olympic Village and the canoe and kayak facilities are abandoned, and the baseball stadium is unused since the Games ended. At least 20 venues lie unused in a sad Olympic legacy of abandoned sport venues.

Athens had its particular problems situated in an economy suffering from recession and enforced fiscal frugality, especially since 2010. But even in Beijing there are Olympic ruins. The baseball stadium was demolished and the site is now home to stray dogs. People preparing for driving tests use the empty space around the closed cycling stadium. The kayak site is filled with stagnant water, the beach volleyball site lies shuttered, and the unused rowing facility overflows with fetid water. The widely praised Bird's Nest stadium is used rarely and costs $11 million a year to maintain. In Turin, the Olympic Village was taken over by squatters and then became a site for migrants and refugees. In Sochi, many of the venues of the 2014 Winter Games sit abandoned and underused.

Part of the problem is what to do with highly specific venues built for Olympic sports that have little local interest? The golf course in Rio lies empty not only because of the financial squeeze in the country, but also because golf is not a popular sport in Rio. Individual venues for unpopular sports in eccentric locations are rarely used after the Olympic athletes have gone home.

A much better post-Olympic legacy comes from smaller venues that have greater adaptability. The massive stadium that can easily house 80,000 people and looks so good during the Games is difficult to fill on a regular basis after the Games leave town. Smaller, more-flexible 20,000-person venues can be used to host a range of athletic and non-athletic events.

Post-Games privatization can solve some of the problems. The Centennial Olympic Stadium of the 1996 Atlanta Games was designed so that it turned into a baseball field at the end of the Games. The soccer stadium for the 2004 Athens Games with 32,000 capacity reverted to home ground for one of the two main professional soccer teams in the capital, Olympiacos. It is well connected to public transport and the stadium contains an entire shopping mall. While both these cases provide example of positive post-Games usage, they also raise concerns about the use of public money to aid private corporations and companies.

Lavish spending on short-term events is not an efficient use of resources. Olympic venues cost a great deal of money to build and maintain, and there is now a vast legacy of abandoned and underused athletic venues, a cruel reminder of the problems of how to effectively use expensive venues after the national anthems have stopped playing. The conclusion is that building venues does not necessarily leave a positive legacy. They need to be carefully planned with post-Games usage in mind, and they need to be integrated into the fabric of the city and local culture. And, again, these are not issues that concern the IOC. They are focused on getting the venues for the sports of the Games. Any post-Games legacy is a bonus for the city, not a real or binding requirement for a city seeking to host the Games.

Sites

Since 2002, the IOC has encouraged more-compact Olympic Games, with venues more concentrated in an urban environment. In the US internal competition to host the 2012 Games, San Francisco lost out because its bid did not conform to this new IOC standard.

There is an emerging pattern of multi-clusters with a concentration of activity in one main site: examples include Parc Olympique in Montreal,

Parc de Montjuic in Barcelona, Homebush Bay in Sydney, Queen Elizabeth Olympic Park in London, and Barra da Tijuca in Rio. The problem is that a massive site with large expansive public spaces designed to cope with thousands of visitors in a short period of time can subsequently fall idle, too large for the reduced post-Games usage. Even Barcelona, widely praised for the careful integration of hosting the Games with a longer-term urban redevelopment plan, has a main site, Parc de Montjuic, that sits strangely idle and half empty in an otherwise crowded and lively city (Figure 7.2). The Ramblas it is not. And the post-Games Olympic Park in London is still underwhelming.

Many major Olympics sites are vast open spaces that have a sense of emotional dereliction. Too big to be easily stitched into the fabric of city, they represent a huge space to maintain and difficult to use efficiently and effectively after the Games have ended. Built to house hundreds of thousands, the main Olympics site in Beijing, Rio, Montreal, Sydney, and Athens, for example, are rarely used to full capacity and are a net drain of resources. Consider Sydney, where the two main Olympic stadiums experienced post-Games major revenue shortfalls caused by competition from other smaller stadiums and a lack of major sporting events. The Olympic Park at Homebush Bay did not live up to expectations or pre-Games plans.

Figure 7.2 Legacies: Parc de Montjuic, Barcelona, Spain
Source: John Rennie Short

Although a designated train line was built, the site is physically isolated from the wider city. As one study concluded, "Ten years after the Olympic Games the Olympic Park is still simply an appendage to the city and does not serve as the intended amalgam for the integrated metropolitan region."[8]

The main site of the Athens Olympics costs close to $500,000 per year in just the basic maintenance of heating, cooling, lighting, and security. It will take 30 years to pay off the cost of building the Bird's Nest in Beijing and it costs $19 million a year in combined maintenance debt repayments. The stadium will be used for the opening and closing ceremonies of the 2022 Winter Games. Authorities are seeking to sell the naming rights to offset costs.

The massively expensive sporting facilities concentrated in large expansive central sites necessary to host the Games are often underutilized and expensive to maintain after the Games have ended.

Hosting the Games is a difficult proposition. Widely dispersing the venues can make them inaccessible during and after the Games, but concentrating many of them means creating a space for thousands of visitors for only two weeks that is difficult to utilize effectively and economically in the post-Games era. The two-week vibrant large public space can soon become eerily empty, socially desolate, and disturbingly underused.

Security: the unspoken legacy

The Olympic Games create the need and provide the opportunity for more-advanced security systems, increased surveillance, and the greater securitization of urban public space.[9]

After the 1972 Munich Games, there was new emphasis on threat and security during the Games. This emphasis took various forms, including more-fortified Olympic architecture, more overt policing and often a military presence, and the isolation of main venues from the everyday life of the city. The security aspect was heightened after 9/11, when a security complex grew and blossomed in cities around the world. Hosting the Olympic Games, a prime terrorist target as the most-global and -televised event, became a platform for new and advanced forms of securing and militarizing a city. New forms of enclosure, social cleansing, and exclusion now permeate host cities, all with the justification of 'security.' During the Games, there is often a criminalization of poverty. Street sweeps and changes in access to public space in the lead-up to and during the Games are used to 'clean' the streets of the poor and indigent. These sweeps constitute an assault on the rights of the more-marginal of the population. From democratic to more authoritarian societies, it is a similar picture: legislation in

Sydney about use of public space, full citizenship in Beijing compromised by hosting the 2008 Games, and homeless youth being further marginalized by Olympic security in Vancouver.[10]

Hosting the Games now provides a test bed for new and permanent forms of urban securitization. New security measures were introduced in Sydney for the 2000 Games. While some of the measures were dropped after the Games, others remain on the books, including the right of the Australian federal government to use the military inside the country without the permission of the states. There is a legacy of restricted civil rights and increased policing and surveillance by the state.

Hosting the Games now leaves as legacy a militarization of urban public space, an infrastructure of upgraded surveillance, security and policing systems, and renewed emphasis on territorial control of urban public space, as well as the more direct use of military personnel, equipment, and technologies. In one sense, the post-Games city is more securitized and militarized, with less freedom of movement than the pre-Games city. The Games are used to upgrade and expand existing security infrastructure to create a super-panopticon of a repository of enhanced security practices: a significant legacy to host cities that is rarely discussed by the IOC.

The games as urban makeover

Hosting the Olympic Games is an expensive opportunity to literally reshape the city and modernize much of the city's infrastructure.

The early Games of the modern era involved few new venues and little new infrastructure, and so the possibility of an urban makeover was limited. An exception was the 1928 Games in Amsterdam, where the Olympic stadium was built on the southern edge of the city as part of an overall plan of urban expansion and revisioning of the city. It was an early but isolated example of using the Games to renew and re-orient the city.

Later, urban change resulted from the frenzy of uncoordinated building projects and infrastructural upgrades. The 1960 Games in Rome saw widened roads, some new stadia, and cleaned up ancient monuments. Tokyo 1964 experienced a $2.8 billion construction bonanza involving a rebuilding of the sewer system, four new five-star hotels, and major transit improvements, including 100 km. of new superhighways, two new subway lines, the Shinkansen bullet train, and a 21-km. monorail that linked the refurnished airport with the downtown.

In Mexico in 1968, only a few stadiums were built but the city did embark on a new metro project. It opened in 1969, a year after the Games ended. For the 1988 Games, the government of South Korea allocated $4 billion for the construction of stadia, new telecommunications, and transport improvements. Seoul expanded its airport, built three new subway lines, and cleaned up the polluted Han River. Barcelona became the most positive model of urban transformation as it employed detailed plans, decades in the making, to host the 1992 Games. Barcelona enlarged its airport and built a new ring road and 35 km. of highways. The city's plans also involved creation of 5 km. of new public beaches, a new waterfront, and the upgrading of an older industrial area of the city, as well as making numerous improvements throughout the metro area, including new roads, a new sewer system, and the creation or improvement of more than 200 parks, plazas, and streets. Old docks and railway yards were turned into revitalized permanent public spaces. The Olympic Village was built in El Poblenou, an area on the coast long dominated by abandoned industrial sites. The makeover involved the demolition of these old buildings as well as the construction of new retail sites, hotels, and office space. Since 1992 the area has attracted more middle-income households and has become one of the new growth areas of the city (Figure 7.3).

The Olympics offered Barcelona the opportunity to make great changes in its physical appearance as city leaders undertook numerous large urban projects: Montjuic Stadium, the Olympic Village, and the Contemporary Art Museum were accompanied by many smaller urban projects designed

Figure 7.3 Legacies: Improved seafront in Barcelona, Spain
Source: John Rennie Short

to "green" the city and make it more pedestrian friendly. The dramatic architectural and planning changes undertaken in Barcelona earned the city the 1999 gold medal from the Royal Institute of British Architects, the first time that the award was given to a city rather than to an individual architect.

For the 2000 Games, Sydney built a new road linking the airport to the downtown and constructed the main venue on a contaminated inner-ring site. Athens spent close to $16 billion in large-scale public investments in water supply, mass transit, and airport connections to get ready for the 2004 Games. Beijing undertook a building frenzy with an estimated $40 billion of Olympic-related buildings and infrastructure, including a new expressway and ring roads, miles of rail and subway tracks, and a $2.2 billion new airport the largest in the world.

The Olympic Games provide both the opportunity and the deadline to implement long-held redevelopment plans. In Greece, for example, the rest of the country had long resisted national investments in Athens. The international showcase of the Olympics provided the necessary spur.

In some cases, the legacies are mixed. In the case of Athens for example, there was a positive physical legacy: the city was able to build a modern transport system, reduce air pollution, renovate parts of the city center, and upgrade parts of the outlying Attica district. However, the largely negative view of the organization and massive cost overruns did not enhance the reputational legacy of the city in the wider world.

The greening of the city

When the IOC decided, after the 1988 Games, to promote greener, more environmentally friendly Olympic Games, cities had to tailor their bids to appear 'greener.' The IOC now requires all candidates to complete an environmental assessment. Sydney won the right to host the 2000 Games in part because its bid placed greater emphasis on urban reuse and brownfield developments rather than on new build and greenfield developments. The main venue was the former abandoned waste site of Homebush Bay. The Sydney Games were part of a wider urban remediation and greening project, and solar panels provided energy to the Olympic Village.

A green Games now intersects with a more general global imaginary of a green city. Not to be green is now similar to being an industrial city, a sign of the past compared to the future, the old in contrast to the new, the premodern as opposed to the postmodern. A green city is closer to the unfolding future than to the disappearing past. To be considered a green city, despite all the ambiguities and difficulties in actualizing such a term, is to be seen as being globally competitive. Beijing's continuing air pollution, despite all the massive efforts to minimize it for the Games, literally and metaphorically cast a pall over the city.

The temporary and permanent greening of the city is now a possibility through hosting the Games. Among the positive effects of recent Games are the clean-up of derelict and abandoned sites, the creation of attractive public space, and even an increase in the environmental quality of the city. Centennial Park is a well-used facility in downtown Atlanta, a direct result of hosting the 1996 Games. In Athens, the Games allowed the reclamation and clean-up of disused quarries, waste dumps, and old army barracks. To reduce air pollution, the organizers of the Beijing Games closed almost 200 factories and 680 mines, and undertook an extensive reforestation program. Beijing also upgraded its public transportation and replaced its old 18,000-bus fleet with more fuel-efficient and fewer polluting vehicles. The city government spent $13 billion on environmental clean-up.

Longer-term effects

The Olympic Games also have a longer-term effect on the city. The city is permanently transformed by the spatial restructuring of hosting the Games. In Seoul, the Chamsil area was redeveloped, in Barcelona the seafront was opened up, and in Atlanta there was a central city gentrification that involved the construction of lofts, hotels and high tech offices. In Sydney, Home Bush Bay was cleaned up. There is also the physical legacy of the Olympic Villages constructed to house the athletes. In Seoul, Barcelona, and Sydney, new Olympic Villages were built and became new neighborhoods. Perhaps the largest infrastructural legacy is the upgrade of airports, telecommunications, mass transit schemes, and road networks that quite literally better connect the city to global flows of people, ideas, and commerce.

The Olympics provide an opportunity to make a global city. Before the Olympics, Athens lacked coherent development plans; it was a disorganized capital popularly represented as a city on the verge of suffocating in its own chaotic growth. The renovation of the seafront, the organization of the historic center, the improved transport system, the cooperation between public and private agencies, and the new use of metropolitan-wide government all became possible. Hosting the Olympics provided the opportunity for citywide, coherent planning to create a modern city. But modernity can come at a cost. The Chinese government used the 2008 Games as an opportunity to modernize Beijing. One plan involved the destruction of the old, high-density neighborhoods of small alleyways in the central part of the city, seen by officials as a remnant of a premodern past. Almost 20 square km. were destroyed and almost 580,000 people were displaced in this one program.

Winter games

At first blush, the Winter Olympic Games do not seem like a useful platform for urban renewal. But they have grown in size, with a tendency toward siting in large cities. The Winter Games now have a substantial urban impact.[11]

The first Winter Games were small, but there has been a gradual shift toward siting the games in major centers of population and using them to regenerate urban and regional economies. There was also the development interest. The successful bid of Squaw Valley to host the 1960 Games was driven by a real estate developer Alexander Cushing, who made a fortune from raising land values and generating more tourism.

The Winter Games in Grenoble (1968) and Sapporo (1972) were used as a form of state regional policy. Grenoble spent 20 percent of the total budget on roads and the Olympic Village became part of an enlarged university. Sapporo spent only 5 percent on sports venues, the rest was spent on 200 km. of new road, a tram system, and two new airports. Nagano 1998 was hard to reach from Tokyo, but that was before the Olympic spending of $19 billion on a bullet train and mountain expressways. Not all Winter Games followed such a massive intervention model. Lillehammer in 1994 was designed as a smaller-scale, more-sustainable project. But Nagano rather than Lillehammer is the dominant model for the modern Winter Games.

Since 2002, there was a shift toward an explicit legacy. Turin 2006 involved the makeover of an old industrial city. The indirect costs included development on brownfields along a new north-south avenue that involved the undergrounding of a railway line and the construction of a six-lane highway. The goal was to reconnect the two halves of the city and provide a new urban centrality. The Games allowed the modernization of some of Turin's infrastructure, reconnected various parts of the city, created a new central spine, the remediation of former polluted sites, and connected the city to the wider Alpine regions through train and road investments.[12]

The Vancouver Games facilitated transport links between the airport and downtown, and between the city and the ski resort of Whistler. It also involved the displacement of 1,400 lower-income housing units in the Eastside neighborhood in the lead-up to the Games, reinforcing a trend toward gentrification in the marginal area close to downtown.[13]

Like the Summer Games, the Winter Games are now used as part of wider urban transformations and regional planning initiatives. However, the environmental impacts of the Winter Games are sometimes more obvious, since they are often held in fragile pristine environments where the human impact is obvious. While the IOC adopted a more sustainable agenda, there are no standard metrics that allow the impact of the Games to be compared, and the IOC takes no financial responsibility for achieving environmental goals.

Impact of recent games

The more recent the Olympic Games, the less our ability to accurately assess long-term benefits. However, we can estimate the short- and medium-term legacy. Let us consider the three most recent Games of London, Sochi, and Rio.

London

The main site of the 2012 London Games was the Lower Lea Valley in East London, and despite being only 7 km. from central London it was a long-ignored part of the city with little public or private investment. The area was a black hole, attracting little attention as the other parts of the city witnessed massive changes. With brownfield sites and a large number of older small businesses, it was not the smart new city of global London. It was a remaining fragment of an older industrial city, gritty and shabby, still home to people and businesses, but with a location that made it susceptible to speculative investment. It did not fit into the image of a bright new postindustrial, financial services city. But the underinvestment and its urban location made it a space of opportunity. It was site ripe for gentrification and speculative development.

For the 2012 Games, polluted waterways and contaminated sites were cleaned up and a 500-acre site was carved out to make the largest urban park in the Europe. At least 4,000 residents were relocated, 300 business were closed, and 14,000 jobs lost.

The Games were a vehicle for the redevelopment of this long-ignored part of East London. In terms of longer-term impacts, the area was revalorized with public and private investments and wired into the wider city with better transport linkages. The area was reintegrated into a citywide real estate, land and housing markets. It was a property-led scheme to recapitalize a black hole of contemporary urban capitalism.[14]

Legacies include turning the main Olympic sites into Queen Elizabeth Olympic Park, and, with new transport links, a possible anchor probably for the construction of more luxury apartments. The Olympic Village was turned into apartments, with 49 percent affordable housing. Almost 10,000 new residential units are planned to be built by 2030. The plan to have up to 40 percent affordable units in the new housing projects was reduced to 20 percent in order to pay back debts. Of the five towers already constructed by developers, only 8 percent have affordable housing. There is little legacy of affordable housing.

And in a pattern reminiscent of Atlanta and Athens, the Olympic stadium became the home of a professional soccer team, West Ham United, after two rounds of bidding. Under a very favorable deal, the football club paid only

15 million pounds toward a 272 million pound post-Olympics refurbishment and was only charged 2.5 million pounds a year on a 99-year lease, with many of the recurring costs of running the stadium to be picked up by the UK taxpayer.[15] The venue also hosts concerts and athletic events.

Sochi

Sochi hosted the 2012 Games. It was the most expensive Winter Games, amounting to almost $55 billion, with 90 percent from the public purse. The aim was twofold: to present a modern face of a successful and powerful Russia to the outside world, a Russia that had weathered the collapse of the Soviet Union and was once again a world power deserving respect. The Games were also employed as a regional policy initiative to turn Sochi into a world-class resort.

There were two main sites: the coastal cluster in Sochi where ice rinks and stadia were built, and the mountain site where many of the outdoor events, such as downhill skiing, took place.

The coastal cluster of the Olympic Park is still vastly underused and annual subsidies of $1.2 billion are required to maintain and operate venues and associated infrastructure. The $10 billion railways connection that links Sochi with the airport and the winter sports areas, with one of the highest per-km construction costs, has so far proved a failure, with just six trains a day. Tourism has improved largely through domestic tourism as a depreciating ruble made foreign travel more expensive for Russians. But foreign tourism faded after the Russian annexation of Crimea.

There was obvious waste and corruption. The government funnels state resources to specific regions through a 'closed system,' with little public input or accountability, that creates numerous corruption opportunities that benefitted a small elite group with close ties to the Kremlin. The lack of transparency was heightened by the scale and speed of the Olympics project.[16] Some take a more optimistic line, seeing obvious waste and corruption but withholding a verdict on the long-term legacy and noting that internal tourism is up from 3.7 million in 2006 to 6.5 million in 2017.[17] The city of Sochi is now a year-round destination for Russian tourists and has played host to many international events, such as Formula One racing. The stadium used for the opening and closing ceremonies of the 2014 Winter Games will host soccer matches in the 2018 World Cup.

Rio

The Rio Games were part of a global repositioning of Brazil. The country wanted to host both the World Cup and the Summer Olympics. The bids were made when the economy was booming, commodity prices were soaring, and there was a real sense of Brazil being part of a new geo-economic bloc of BRICS (Brazil, Russia, India, China, and South Africa), large countries with impressive enough growth rates to rupture the traditional dominance of the US and Western Europe. The reality proved rather more dismal. The 2014 World Cup had massive cost overruns, logistical headaches, and even worse for the national psyche, the national soccer team was humiliated in front of a home crowd in a devastating 7–1 loss to Germany. It was not a good omen for the Summer Games.

The Rio games, like the World Cup before, became an opportunity to gain control over marginal areas. Favelas were thinned out, with residents relocated. Four thousand people were removed from the main site at Barra da Tijuca, part of the 77,000 displaced in the city. The Games allowed the state to exert control over areas formerly only at the edges of government control. The liminal and marginal were reintegrated into formal control.[18]

There was a lot of negative publicity. During the Games, globally relayed images of polluted pools and displaced favela dwellers did little to enhance the city's image, despite the staggeringly beautiful landscape shots favored by the TV producers. The Games tainted the reputation of the city. Post-Games, the negative publicity continued. The OCOG ran out of money and was reduced to bartering with suppliers in order to pay off the swollen debt. The Rio governor, Sergio Cabral, who led the bid to host the 2016 Games, was arrested in November 2016 for being part of cabal that made $66 million in bribes from construction companies in return for state government contracts.

The physical legacy was disappointing. Sports infrastructure crumbled less than a year after the Games ended. A monument to poor planning and corruption Rio, stands as a polar opposite from Barcelona in terms of how to organize a Games to benefit the local inhabitants. Many sites have been abandoned. The Olympic Park is in a poor state, with venues boarded and barricaded, half demolished and pools filled with dirt. The golf course lies neglected. All over the city, Olympic sites are abandoned and boarded up, filled with rubbish and weeds.

The core facilities were built in Barra da Tijuca, 45 minutes from downtown and planned to become part of a wealthy gated community. Low-income residents at the edge of site were evicted. Valuable wetlands were concreted over. For Rio and many other cities, the Games acted as a gentrification on steroids as neoliberalism in all its destructive and regressive glory turned the city's attention from welfare to wealth promotion.[19] Public funds were diverted from education, drug rehabilitation, and poverty reduction and used to lubricate rampant property speculation.

The 31 tower athletes' village turned into luxury apartments by real estate tycoons is, at the time of writing in 2017, less than 10 percent sold. Few of the plans to turn venues into amenity for the local neighborhoods and the wider city amenities have come to fruition, as poor planning is compounded by the financial crisis of the country, state, and city. Private companies were unable to afford the venues and are now in the hands of cash-starved public authorities.[20]

Rio's development was shaped by real estate and construction interests in alliance with their political cronies. There was poor management and rampant corruption. The city and the country was enveloped in a growing financial and political crisis just as the Games were occurring. But even if the Games had been more successful, what would success have looked like? The creation of a wealthy enclave and the enrichment of property and construction companies. In other words, the legacy would have reinforced an increasing inequality in an already unequal city. And it all came with massive price tab. The Rio Games cost $20 billion and will return no more than $4.5 billion. The Games caused massive population displacements, led to rampant property speculation, sullied the reputation of the city, reinforced inequalities, and left little of a positive legacy.

Mega-event syndrome

Rather than thinking of how the city benefits from hosting the Olympic Games, we need to consider the event as an illness that afflicts the city. Martin Müller identifies what he refers to as mega-event syndrome, a group of symptoms that include overpromising benefits, underestimating costs, shifting urban planning priorities to fit the event, using public resources for private interest, and suspending the regular rule of law.[21]

The Games allow a city to showcase itself to a global audience. For two weeks, the city is constantly mentioned and represented in the world's media and the severe deadline overcomes resistances to long-delayed urban makeovers. But hosting the Games demands major urban infrastructural investment and new or expensively upgraded sporting venues that crowd out other forms of public investment, such as spending on education and social welfare, that may serve better the long-term needs of ordinary citizens. Only two Games, both in Los Angeles, have ever made a real profit. Other costs include the dislocation in the city during the construction period. There are also social and environmental costs. The staging of the last 20 Olympic Games displaced 20 million people, including the displacement of almost 750,000 people for the Seoul Games, and 30,000 – predominantly African Americans – for the Atlanta Games. More than 1.25 million people were displaced for the Beijing Games.[22]

The syndrome comes at a tremendous cost for the host city. The 2012 London games cost the organizers $14.6 billion, with more than $4.4 from

British taxpayers. The costs of the Rio 2016 Games, initially projected at $2.3 billion, are closer to $15 billion . . . and counting.

In official bids, there is the overestimation of benefits and the underestimation of costs, with substantial differences between initial estimates and actual spending. There is an intentional low-balling of official bids and the generation of official and semi-official cost-benefit analyses are more sensitive to benefits than to costs. The costs are always higher due to this deliberate underestimation as well as the fixed deadlines and unforeseen events. The extra costs are then borne by public authorities, while much of subsequent the revenues and benefits are privatized by private or nonprofit organizations that are neither democratically elected nor publicly accountable. And to add insult to injury hosting the Games means limitations on citizens' rights and the free use of urban public space. The Games leave as legacy a more securitized and militarized city.

Conclusions

To briefly summarize. As the cost and criticisms have mounted, the Games are more and more defended as a positive catalyst that create a long-lasting legacy. Never mind the cost, look at the shiny new metro system.

To be fair, there are some examples of a positive legacy. Barcelona upgraded its city for the majority of the citizenry by integrating long-term plans with the contingence of getting ready for the 1992 Games. The Barcelona model has rarely been replicated. At best, host cities have legacies of global reputations, better transport links, improved venues, and urban regeneration. Rarely do cities have of all of them.

At worst, there are negative legacies of tarnished reputations, venues that turn to ruins, Olympic Parks that lie half-empty, and transport systems that do little more than connect the city to the airport, making life easier for the international traveler but not necessarily easier for the everyday commuter. The Olympic legacy rarely lives up to the promises.

The legacy argument is problematic even when positive. Assume the money was spent directly on transport and urban makeovers without hosting the Games. A city would get the same effect, with some added features. First, the city would not have the risk of reputational failure. Even when successful, the reputations of successful host cities are rarely improved enough to attract extra investments and tourists.

Second, the city would avoid the operational costs of hosting the Games that are not insignificant. In Sochi, for example, sports-related spending amounted to $16.1 billion. The Games impose large administrative costs; they have to be planned and organized. That requires administrative capacity and expertise. The Games reinforces government powers without enhancing their capacity.

Third, the city would not have to build venues that are little used after the Games. The legacy argument is undermined by the need for costly venues maintained by host cities that too often lie empty, shuttered, or under used.

Fourth, the infrastructure legacy is often compromised by the need to make investments for a unique, once-in-a-generation two-week event rather than concentrating on long-term needs. Why not miss out on the Games and make strategic investments directly toward the economic efficiency of the city and the good of all the residents? If urban renewal is the goal, then this could be more efficiently and cheaply expedited with targeted investment without needing to provide a baseball stadium, white-water complexes, or velodromes that may lack users and spectators and generate debts and maintenance costs for years to come.

Fifth, the nature of the Games – a global event with hard deadlines and limited time to get ready – can lead to hurried constructions, poor planning, and unforeseen events that rack up costs. The plans for the 2004 Athens Games had to be changed at the last minute in response to community and environmental groups. The strategic goal of redeveloping parts of the seafront had to be abandoned and reinforced the dispersion of the venues, making their post-Games use even more difficult after the 2010 fiscal crisis of the state.

And since venues have to be built at specific times, it is impossible to spread out the borrowing and construction costs. Once a city is committed to hosing the Games, they have to find the money immediately at rates that can be higher than usual. Cost overruns are endemic to hosting the games. The tight deadline can easily lead to price gouging, sweetheart deals, corruption, and things simply costing much more than they need to. Hosting the Games adds an unnecessary premium to all infrastructure costs and leaves a legacy of debt. Servicing the Olympic debt for Sochi costs the government $4 billion year, wiping out any economic benefits of the Games.

Finally, the peculiar natures of the arrangement in which the IOC, OCOG, and state authorities are involved, often involves secret discussions and priority setting, thereby undermining the democratic process. Major investments are made with little public input. Formal planning procedures or environmental impact statements are often avoided or ignored. The system heightens the possibility of rigged bids, engineered tenders, cronyism, and corruption.

In other words, the Games are a rushed, expensive, half-planned, half-IOC-dictated urban makeover that lack transparency and accountability. They add a price premium because the host city could make all the long-term legacies through more carefully targeted objectives without having to meet the requirement of an unelected self-interested IOC and the peculiar nature of a globally televised two-week event – and at much less cost, with more public accountability and greater transparency. On closer examination, the legacy argument is simply a legitimizing cover for an expensive mega-event with high costs, dubious benefits, and uncertain outcomes.

We end with a sobering note. As two researchers, one of them better known for highlighting the positive impacts of hosting the Games, so not the usual critic, noted:

> It remains the case that the scientific evidence needed to evaluate the economic importance of the legacy of hosting major sports events, such as the Olympic Games, simply does not exist.[23]

We would need good quality data over at least 20 years, scrupulous analysis, and a willingness to objectively measure the net legacy benefits. In lieu of this, arguments for hosting the Games are based on fantasies of legacy rather than on any real assessment of legacies.

Notes

1 Tomlinson, A. (2014) Olympic legacies: Recurrent rhetoric and hard realities. *Contemporary Social Science* 9: 137–158.
2 Brunet, F. (2005). *The Economic Impact of the Barcelona Olympic Games, 1986–2004: Barcelona: The Legacy of the Games, 1992–2002.* Barcelona: Centre d'Estudis Olímpics UAB. http://olympicstudies.uab.es/pdf/wp084_eng.pdf
3 Kim, J., Kang, J. H., and Kim, Y.-K. (2014) Impact of mega sport events on destination image and country image. *Sport Marketing Quarterly* 23: 161–175.
4 Kassens-Noor, E. (2013) Transport legacy of the Olympic Games 1992–2012. *Journal of Urban Affairs* 35: 393–416.
5 Kassens-Noor, E. (2012) *Planning Olympic Legacies: Transport Dreams and Urban Realities.* London and New York: Routledge.
6 Kassens-Noor, E. (2015) The legacy of the 2004 Olympic for the Athens transport system. In *Routledge Handbook of Sport and Legacy: Meeting the Challenge of Major Sports Events* (pp. 131–141). London: Routledge.
7 Knowlton, E. (2015) What abandoned Olympic venues from around the world look like today. *Business Insider.* http://www.businessinsider.com/abandoned-olympic-venues-around-the-world-photos-2015-8
8 Yamawaki, Y. and Duarte, F. (2014) Olympics and legacy in Sydney: Urban transformation and real estate a decade after the Games. *Journal of Urban Design* 19: 511–540. Quote p. 28.
9 Boyle, P. and Haggerty, K. D. (2009) Spectacular security: Mega-events and the security complex. *International Political Sociology* 3: 257–274.
10 Toohey, K. and Taylor, T. (2012) Surveillance and securitization: A forgotten Sydney Olympic legacy. *International Review for the Sociology of Sport* 47: 324–337.
   Kennelly, J. and Watt, P. (2011) Sanitizing public space in Olympic host cities: The spatial experiences of marginalized youth in 2010 Vancouver and 2012 London. *Sociology* 45: 765–781.

92   Urban legacies

Klauser, F. R. (2015) Interacting forms of expertise and authority in mega-event security: The example of the 2010 Vancouver Olympic Games. *Geographical Journal* 181: 224–234.

Shin, H. B. and Bingqin, L. (2013) Whose games? The costs of being "Olympic citizens" in Beijing. *Environment and Urbanization*. http://eprints.lse.ac.uk/52676/1/Shin_Whose_games_costs_2013.pdf

11 Essex, S. and De Groot, J. (2016) The Winter Olympics; Driving urban change, 1924–2022. In Gold, J. and Gold, M. (eds.), *Olympic Cities: City Agendas, Planning and the World's Games, 1896–2020* (pp. 64–89). London: Routledge.

12 Dansero, E. and Mela, A. (2012) Bringing the mountains into the city: Legacy of the Winter Olympics, Turin 2006. In *The Palgrave Handbook of Olympic Studies* (pp. 178–194). New York: Palgrave Macmillan.

13 Kennelly, J. (2017) Symbolic violence and the Olympic Games: Low-income youth, social legacy commitments, and urban exclusion in Olympic host cities. *Journal of Youth Studies* 20: 145–161.

14 Wagg, S. (2015) *The London Olympics of 2012: Politics, Promises and Legacy.* London: Palgrave Macmillan.

15 Gibson, O. (2016) How West Ham struck the deal of the century with Olympic stadium move. *The Guardian.* www.theguardian.com/football/2016/apr/14/west-ham-deal-century-olympic-stadium

16 Müller, M. (2014) After Sochi 2014: Costs and impacts of Russia's Olympic Games. *Eurasian Geography and Economics* 55: 628–655.

Orttung, R. W. and Zhemukhov, S. (2014) The 2014 Sochi Olympic mega-project and Russia's political economy. *East European Politics* 30: 175–191.

17 Golubchikov, O. (2016) *The 2014 Sochi Winter Olympics: who stands to gain?* In: Transparency International, ed. *Global Corruption Report: Sport*, Abingdon: Routledge, pp. 183–191. http://orca.cf.ac.uk/86672/1/2016-3.10_SochiWhoGains_Golubchikov_GCRSport.pdf

Filipov, D. (2017) Sochi: A $50 billion dream come true? *The Washington Post*, November 16: p. A12.

18 Freeman, J. (2014) Raising the flag over Rio de Janeiro's favelas: Citizenship and social control in the Olympic city. *Journal of Latin American Geography* 13: 7–38.

19 Zimbalist, A. (ed.) (2017) *Rio 2016: Olympic Myths and Hard Realities.* Washington, DC: Brookings Institution Press.

20 The Guardian (2017) Rio Olympics venues already falling into a state of disrepair. www.theguardian.com/sport/2017/feb/10/rio-olympic-venues-already-falling-into-a-state-of-disrepair

21 Müller, M. (2015) The mega-event syndrome: Why so much goes wrong in mega-event planning and what to do about it. *Journal of the American Planning Association* 81: 6–17.

22 Centre on Housing Rights and Evictions (2007) *Fair Play for Housing Rights: Mega-Events, Olympic Games and Housing Rights.* Geneva: Centre on Housing Rights and Evictions. www.ruig-gian.org/ressources/Report%20Fair%20Play%20FINAL%20FINAL%20200070531.pdf

23 Gratton, C. and Preuss, H. (2008) Maximizing Olympic impacts by building up legacies. *The International Journal of the History of Sport* 25: 1922–1938. p. 1933.

8   Alternatives to event capture

Event capture

In many discussions of the Olympic Games, it is assumed that a city wins the right to host the event. We need to replace the notion of a city winning the Games with the image of the Games capturing a city.[1] As a metaphor for the Games as parasitic on the host cities consider the European common cuckoo, a species of bird that lays its eggs in the nest of other birds. The

Figure 8.1 Event Capture: With huge direct costs, a legacy of debt that persisted for decades, and a barely used main Olympics site unconnected to the life of the city, Montreal 1976 is the prime example of the event capture of a city

Source: John Rennie Short

cuckoo egg hatches earlier than the existing eggs, grows faster, and evicts the legitimate brood. The unsuspecting parent birds then unwittingly care for the sole cuckoo chick. The Games are the cuckoo egg, the host city is the nest, and the taxpayers are like the parent birds, responsible for the rearing and caring of an intruder.

Soaring costs are baked into the city selection process. The competition is designed to force cities to bid ever upward, proposing state-of-the-art projects that they might not even need.

A mounting crisis

It is clear that the Olympic Games are in something of a crisis. The recent Winter and Summer Olympic Games in Sochi and Rio did little to enhance the reputation of the Games. Costs continue to rise, there is growing resistance from communities in bid and host cities, and the narrative frame has changed toward a much more critical gaze on the IOC and the hosting of the Games. The spiraling costs and fiscal uncertainty have made some cities shy away from bidding, or even withdrawing their bids. The 2022 Winter Games had only two bids, from Beijing and Almaty, Kazakhstan. Norway pulled out and publicized the extravagant claims made by the IOC. If there are fewer bid cities and only the more authoritarian societies bid to host the Games, then the entire Olympic brand becomes tarnished.

Bidding for the 2024 Games saw significant defections. In 2015, Boston pulled out. In November 2015, a slight majority of residents of Hamburg voted to pull out of the bidding process. Less than a year later, at a press conference held on the Spanish Steps on Sept. 23, 2016, the mayor of Rome, Virginia Raggi, announced to the world that the Eternal City did not want to be considered as a host city for the 2024 Olympic Games. She said the constructions costs and possible future debt encumbrance were too much for a city facing a budget shortfall and already burdened with debt. Her decision was considered a defeat for the Italian Olympic Committee, who, without the support of the city's mayor, quickly abandoned the bid.

Withdrawals like Rome's are becoming more common. Boston, Hamburg, and Budapest all turned their backs on the opportunity to host the 2024 Games – and gave hope, advice, and models to bid resisters all across the globe. Rome's mayor mentioned these other cities in her public announcement on the Spanish Steps. There were only two bids for the 2024 Summer Games: Paris and Los Angeles.

A sense of crisis even pervades the IOC. One attempt at halting the burgeoning size of the Games is a 28–301–10,500 rule: to have no more than 28 sports, 301 medals, and 10,500 athletes for the Summer Games. At the 2016

Rio Games, there were 28 sports, 306 medals (including gold, silver, and bronze), and 11,000 athletes. A 2014 IOC document suggested significant changes.[2] Some of the recommendations relate to costs, bidding, and legacy:

- to actively promote the maximum use of existing facilities and the use of temporary and demountable venues
- to introduce an assistance phase during which cities considering a bid will be advised by the IOC about bid procedures, core Games requirements, and how previous cities have ensured positive bid and Games legacies
- to allow, for the Olympic Games, the organization of entire sports or disciplines outside the host city or, in exceptional cases, outside the host country notably for reasons of geography and sustainability

Others are a response to the declining reputation of the IOC and its Olympic project:

- to make the Host City Contract public
- to include details of the IOC's financial contribution to the OCOG
- to clarify the elements for the two different budgets related to the organization of the Olympic Games: long-term investment in infrastructure and return on such investment on the one hand, and the operational budget on the other hand
- to communicate and promote the contribution of the IOC to the Games
- to pay for costs incurred in relation to the visit of the IOC Evaluation Commission

These are only recommendations and we will have to look to subsequent bids and Games to see if they amount to anything more than rhetoric. However, the recommendations do reveal the depth of the legitimacy crisis for IOC.

The IOC recommendations do not radically change the organization and financing of the Games. The proposals keep the basic franchise and financing model intact.

There is also a debate occurring beyond the IOC. In order to reduce the spiraling costs and declining legitimacy, some suggest that host cities should bargain with the IOC for better conditions, earmark and cap public sector contributions, and seek independent advice on the costs and benefits of mega-events. The IOC, in turn, should reduce the size and requirements of the Games.[3] There are also more radical ideas that lessen the possibility of event capture by undermining the IOC franchise model.

A permanent home

The idea of a permanent home for the Olympic Games is not new. The original Olympics were always held in Olympia, Greece. In 1896, after the very first modern Games, the King of Greece called for the event to be located permanently in his country as a 'peaceful meeting place of all nations.' The American athletic delegation of the day supported the idea, noting that the games should never be removed from their 'native soil.' Coubertin, in contrast, wanted a nomadic Games to diffuse the then-fledgling Olympic idea. He believed that the nascent organization would be renewed and its financing more secure with a changing host city. His plan triumphed. The next Summer Games were held in Paris. The Greeks persisted and even hosted what was referred to as the Second International Olympic Games in 1906, but they never achieved their goal of a permanent Greek site for the Summer Games. Coubertin's vision of a nomadic Games triumphed.

The idea of a permanent home resurfaces whenever the traditional model is under serious threat. In 1980, when a series of boycotts and Cold War tensions threatened the legitimacy of Games, one commentator suggested establishing a fixed site for the Summer Games in a neutral country, with a rotation of locations for the Winter Games.[4] When the United States boycotted the 1980 Olympics in Moscow, the US Senate Foreign Relations Committee suggested looking into "the creation of permanent homes for Summer and Winter Olympic Games, including one in Greece, the country of their origin."[5] Even the IOC studied the possibility of a perennial Summer Olympics site on Greece's Peloponnese peninsula. The site was to be granted neutral status by the Greek government, which would provide territory and infrastructure. The IOC and its member states were to fund construction.[6]

The permanent home idea disappeared from view as Cold War tensions evaporated. Global participation and the end of boycotts meant there was no shortage of bid cities. In more recent years, however – with the mounting criticisms, rising costs. and declining support – the idea of a fixed site at least for the Summer Games is revived. The basic argument is that instead of investing billions of dollars for a new host every four years, it would be cheaper and easier to create a permanent Olympic site.[7]

There are enormous infrastructure costs associated with preparing and hosting the Olympics. Most often, the host cities initially do not have the required capacity and the infrastructure. Building and upgrading stadiums, venues, and accommodation for athletes and spectators are some of the things that must be completed. Huge investments are made in construction, which could otherwise be used in other forms of public investment. And with every change of venue, the Olympics reinvents the wheel, fielding a new team of planners, contractors, accountants, technicians, security personnel, and volunteers every four years. The result is increased costs and less efficiency.

Instead of investing billions of dollars for a new city every four years, we could create a permanent Olympic facility. My preference is for a small enclave constituted as international territory, close to the original site of Olympia. This would avoid disruption and social dislocation and eliminate the often-massive costs to citizens in the host cities. Younger athletes, especially from the less-wealthy parts of the world, could train there for years. The site could host international gatherings of young people interested in arts and culture as well as sports. It could be an ongoing experiment in sustainability and responsive architecture, as the reuse and adaption of buildings could provide a model of sustainable urbanism to a wider world. The same site would also standardize the sporting element, providing a stable setting and climate against which to benchmark athletic performances over time.

The IOC is the obvious, if not perhaps the best, organization to be responsible for this scheme. An initial cost of $100 billion could be offset against bonds or loans on the basis of future media revenues. As one of the biggest events on the planet, it would not be difficult to generate funds to cover the initial construction and operating costs. It would mean no renewal of the Barcelona waterfront, the (partial) remediation of Homebush Bay in Sydney, or the lower Lea Valley in London. But for every Barcelona and Sydney, there is also an Atlanta and Beijing, where the poor were displaced and further marginalized.

The very recent Greek crisis provides an opportunity. The Greeks are in hock to around $271 billion to all official lenders. The government in Athens has agreed to transfer state assets of $80 billion to an independent fund. How about selling a permanent site in Greece for the Summer Olympics?

The sale would allow an international zone to be created, provide desperately needed revenue to Greece and some relief for debtors, while the necessary construction could help to stimulate the Greek economy. Having a permanent site for the Summer Olympics would also return the Games to their historic birthplace, and dispense with the fiscal insanity of cities overbidding for the Summer Olympics, leaving themselves with debts and underused infrastructure.

The original Olympics were held in Olympia, Greece, for 800 years. The changing site is a modern phenomenon used to spread support in the early stages of the modern Olympic movement. Support exists now, globally. Why not return the Games to their real roots?

I have argued this position for some time.[8] A permanent site, I believe, would avoid all disruption and social dislocation, and eliminate the often-massive costs to citizens in the host cities.

A fixed site raises the basic issue of location. My preference is for a site in Greece. A tongue-in-cheek argument proposed a separate island home. Proposals in a similar vein argue for Vancouver as a permanent home for both Summer and Winter Olympics,[9] while others argue for Los Angeles as permanent home for the Summer Games, with Winter Games either in Europe or Japan. Proponents of the permanent model are less certain about the preferred site for the Winter Games, although Japan and Switzerland have been mentioned as potential hosts. But these are secondary questions. The main point is to seriously reconsider the nomadic model.

Decentralizing the games

There are also decentralized alternatives. Rather than changing a nomadic site for fixed site, some argue for a decentralizing to multiple sites. This would involve an Olympic Games where different cities simultaneously hosted different athletic events. With a manageable number of athletes in any given site, the event would not overwhelm the local infrastructure or require massive infrastructural investment.

Many cities would be willing to host a single Olympic sport, especially one that was locally popular where the necessary venues were already in place. A decentered Olympics could solve the problem of building new expensive venues that subsequently languish. It would also widen the range of cities able to host Olympic events.

The downside of this solution is that television and corporate sponsors would miss out on the opportunity to maximize their impact. The Games, rather than concentered in one site, would be spread over different cities in different time zones. Television coverage would be much more expensive and global corporate advertising diluted. One suggestion is to have the opening and closing ceremonies in one city.

Another form of decentering would involve a network of cities, either within one country or among countries in the same region. While few individual African cities could host the Summer Olympics, a range of African cities acting as a Games networks for two weeks could host the Games. Similarly, a range of Alpine cities in Europe could successfully host the Winter Games by spreading out the infrastructure load and environmental impacts.

Some propose rotating the Olympics among several cities that recently hosted the Olympics – perhaps choosing five to represent the five interlocking rings of the Olympic symbol – or cycling them through one permanent venue on each continent.[10]

A radical alternative

In many of the discussions of the Olympic Games, it is assumed that there is congruence of interest between the IOC and the host cities. But the game of the Games is rigged, with the IOC bearing no cost but reaping great profits, while the competition seems designed to force cities to bid ever higher. The Olympic bidding process is lucrative for the IOC. Host cities spend billions of dollars to host the event, media-rights deals will continue to grow in value, and the IOC will continue to rake in money. Proposals that undermine the nomadic franchise model are therefore unlikely to get serious consideration from the IOC, which is doing well from the current arrangement, even if most inhabitants of host cities are not.

As long as the IOC keeps control of the Olympics, I do not expect radical change. Their power, influence, and revenue streams rest on their franchise model. They collected roughly $8 billion in revenue from 2008 to 2012. They will resist any moves, such as a permanent home, that undermines their lucrative franchise model.

But it is time for a seismic change. Not just a change in how we host the Games, but who controls the Games. The Olympics are too important and valuable to be left in the hands of the IOC. Their franchise enriches them but provides few long-term positive benefits for the host cities. The physical legacies that work well, and not all of them do, could have been provided for less money, with greater transparency and more public input. Rather than using the Games to rebuild and renew their cities, the third best choice and the bronze medal winner, citizens would be better served by not hosting the Games. Second best choice, the silver medal, is to bid but not win. And the gold medal winner would be to neither bid nor host but to concentrate on planning for a better city. A fairer, more just, and efficient city is best served by neither hosting nor bidding for the Games.

Notes

1 Martin Müller describes this process, he calls it event seizure, as one in which mega-events and the supporting local elites capture a city.
   Müller, M. (2016) How megaevents capture their hosts: event seizure and The World Cup 2018 in Russia. *Urban Geography* 1–20.
2 IOC (2014) Olympic Agenda 2020: 20 + 20 Recommendations. https://stillmed. olympic.org/Documents/Olympic_Agenda_2020/Olympic_Agenda_2020-20-20_Recommendations-ENG.pdf
3 Müller, M. (2015) The mega-event syndrome: Why so much goes wrong in mega-event planning and what to do about it. *Journal of the American Planning Association* 81: 6–17.
4 Atkin, R. (1980) Olympic voices for reform. *Christian Science Monitor*. www. csmonitor.com/1980/0212/021228.html

5 Atkin, R. (1980) Olympic voices for reform. *The Christian Science Monitor*. https://www.csmonitor.com/1980/0212/021228.html
6 McDonald, R. (1980) Greece could become permanent site for Olympics. *The Chicago Tribune*. http://archives.chicagotribune.com/1980/03/09/page/53/article/greece-could-become-permanent-site-of-olympics
7 Short, J. R. (2015) We should host the Olympics in the same place every time. *The Washington Post*. www.washingtonpost.com/posteverything/wp/2015/07/28/we-should-host-the-olympics-in-the-same-place-every-time/
8 Why can't we hold the Olympics in the same place every time. *The Atlantic CityLab*. www.citylab.com/politics/2013/09/two-words-olympics-island/6797/
   Should the Olympic Games have a permanent venue? *The Current (CBC Radio, Canada)*. www.cbc.ca/radio/thecurrent/the-current-for-august-17-2016-1.3724261/should-the-olympic-games-have-a-permanent-venue-1.3724289
   The Olympics need reform. *Forbes*. www.forbes.com/sites/andrewbrennan/2016/08/31/the-olympics-just-like-fifa-and-its-lauded-world-cup-is-a-money-racket-and-needs-reform/#38123eec1804
   The time has come for the Olympic Games to be held in the same venue every four years. *CityAm (London, UK)*. www.cityam.com/247763/time-has-come-olympic-games-held-same-venue-every-four
9 *The Olympics should be in Vancouver. Slate*. www.slate.com/blogs/five_ring_circus/2016/08/05/the_olymics_should_be_in_vancouver_summer_and_winter_forever.html
10 The Editors (2014) Give the Olympics a permanent home. *Bloomberg View*. https://www.bloomberg.com/view/articles/2014-02-05/give-the-olympics-a-permanent-home

A guide to further reading

Here is just a very small sample of the vast and growing literature on the Olympic Games. One indispensable resource is the official IOC site, www. olympic.org/the-ioc. Of special interest is the new Olympic World Library (https://library.olympic.org). From there, you can navigate to the main topics covered in this book, although with perhaps a slightly different interpretation. It is a great source of information and official reports.

Another useful source is the LA84 Foundation Digital Library http://search.la84.org/search?site=default_collection&client=default_frontend&output=xml_no_dtd&proxystylesheet=default_frontend&proxycustom=%3CHOME/%3E

It contains periodicals, proceedings, and official reports of all Olympic Games and a select range of oral histories.

Ancient games

Finley, M. I. and Pleket, H. W. (1976) *The Olympic Games: The First Thousand Years*. London: Chatto and Windus.

Miller, S. G. (1991) *Arete: Greek Sports from Ancient Sources*. Berkeley and Los Angeles: University of California Press.

Perottet, T. (2004) *The Naked Olympics: The True Story of the Ancient Games*. New York: Random.

Swaddling, J. (2015, 3rd ed.) *The Ancient Olympic Games*. London: British Museum Press and University of Texas Press.

Woff, R. (1999) *The Ancient Greek Olympics*. New York: Oxford University Press.

The modern games

Boykoff, J. (2016) *Power Games: A Political History of The Olympics*. London and New York: Verso.

Chappelet, J.-L. and Kubler-Mabbott, B. (2008) *The International Olympic Committee and the Olympic System: The Governance of World Sport*. London and New York: Routledge.

Goldblatt, D. (2016) *The Games: A Global History of the Olympics*. New York and London: W. W. Norton.

Gruneau, R. and Horne, J. (eds.) (2015) *Mega-Events and Globalization: Capital and Spectacle in a Changing World Order*. London: Routledge.

Guttman, A. (2002, 2nd ed.) *The Olympics: A History of The Modern Games*. Urbana and Chicago: University of Illinois Press.

Horne, J. and Whannel, G. (2016, 2nd ed.) *Understanding the Olympics*. London: Routledge.

Lenskyj, H. and Wagg, S. (eds.) (2014) *The Palgrave Handbook of Olympic Studies*. London: Palgrave Macmillan.

O'Mahoney, M. (2012) *Olympic Visions: Images of The Games Through History*. London: Reaktion.

Pound, D. (2004) *Inside the Olympics*. Toronto: Wiley.

Senn, A. E. (1999) *Power, Politics and The Olympic Games*. Champaign, IL: Human Kinetics.

Bidding for the games

Feddersen, A., Maennig, W., and Zimmermann, P. (2007) *How to Win the Olympic Games: The Empirics of Key Success Factors of Olympic Bids*. http://college. holycross.edu/RePEc/spe/FeddersenMaennigZimmermann_OlympicBidding.pdf

Olivier, R. and Lauermann, J. (2017) *Failed Olympic Bids and the Transformation of Urban Space*. London: Palgrave.

Rowe, D. (2012) The bid, the lead-up, the event and the legacy: Global cultural politics and hosting the Games. *British Journal of Sociology* 63: 285–305.

Shoemaker, M. M. (2016) *No More Hats Thrown into the Olympic Rings: An Analysis of the Olympic Bidding Process*. Doctoral dissertation, Boston University. http://dcommon.bu.edu/handle/2144/17696

Surborg, B., VanWynsberghe, R., and Wyly, E. (2008) Mapping the Olympic growth machine: Transnational urbanism and the growth machine diaspora. *City* 12: 341–355.

Economic costs and benefits

Applebaum, B. (2014, August 5th) Does hosting the Games actually pay off? *The New York Times Magazine*. www.nytimes.com/2014/08/10/magazine/does-hosting-the-olympics-actually-pay-off.html?_r=2

Baade, R. A. and Matheson, V. A. (2016) Going for the gold: The economics of the Olympics. *Journal of Economic Perspectives* 30: 201–218.

Flyvbjerg, B. and Stewart, A. (2012) *Olympic Proportions: Cost and Cost Overrun at the Olympics 1960–2012*. Saïd Business School Working Paper, University of Oxford.

Preuss, H. (2004) *The Economics of Staging the Olympics: A Comparison of the Games, 1972–2008*. Cheltenham: Edward Elgar.

Zimbalist, A. (2016, 2nd ed.) *Circus Maximus: The Economic Gamble Behind Hosting the Olympics and World Cup*. Washington, DC: Brookings Institution Press.

Social costs and benefits

Bajc, V. (ed.) (2015) *Securing the Olympics: From Tokyo 1964 to London 2012 and Beyond*. London: Palgrave Macmillan.

Freeman, J. (2014) Raising the flag over Rio de Janeiro's favelas: Citizenship and social control in the Olympic city. *Journal of Latin American Geography* 13: 7–38.

Karamichas, J. (2013) *The Olympic Games and the Environment*. London, UK: Palgrave Macmillan.

Kennelly, J. (2016) *Olympic Exclusions: Youth, Poverty and Social Legacies*. London: Routledge.

Critical perspectives

Barney, R., Wenn, S. R., and Martyn, S. G. (2004) *Selling the Five Rings: The IOC and the Rise of the Olympic Commercialism*. Provo: University of Utah Press.

Boykoff, J. (2014) *Activism and the Olympics: Dissent at the Games in Vancouver and London*. New Brunswick: Rutgers University Press.

Boykoff, J. (2014) *Celebration Capitalism and the Olympic Games*. London: Routledge.

Dempsey, C. and Zimbalist, A. (2017) *No Boston Olympics: How and Why Smart Cities Are Passing on the Torch*. Lebanon, NH: ForeEdge.

Jennings, A. and Sambrook, C. (2000) *The Great Olympic Swindle*. New York: Simon and Schuster.

Lenskyj, H. J. (2008) *Olympic Industry Resistance: Challenging Olympic Power and Propaganda*. Albany: SUNY Press.

Müller, M. (2015) The mega-event syndrome: Why so much goes wrong in mega-event planning and what to do about it. *Journal of the American Planning Association* 81: 6–17.

Shaw, C. A. (2008) *Five Ring Circus: Myths and Realities of the Olympic Games*. Gabriola Island: New Society.

Legacies

Broudehoux, A.-M. (2017) *Mega-events and Urban Image Construction: Beijing and Rio de Janeiro*. London: Routledge.

Coaffee, J. (2015) The uneven geographies of the Olympic carceral: From exceptionalism to normalisation. *The Geographical Journal* 181: 199–211.

Essex, S. and Chalkley, B. (1998) Olympic Games: Catalyst of urban change. *Leisure Studies* 17: 187–206.

Gold, J. R. and Gold, M. M. (2008) Olympic cities: Regeneration, city rebranding and changing urban agendas. *Geography Compass* 2: 300–318.

Gold, J. R. and Gold, M. M. (eds.) (2016, 3rd ed.) *Olympic Cities: City Agendas, Planning and the World's Games, 1896–2020*. London: Routledge.

Kassens-Noor, E. (2012) *Planning Olympic Legacies: Transport Dreams and Urban Realities*. London and New York: Routledge.

Mangan, J. A. and Dyreson, M. (eds.) (2010) *Olympic Legacies: Unintended and Intended.* New York: Routledge.

Morages, M., Kennet, C., and Puig, N. (eds.) (2003) *The Legacy of the Olympic Games 1984–2000.* Lausanne: International Olympic Committee.

Pitts, A. and Liao, H. (2009) *Sustainable Olympic Design and Urban Development.* New York: Routledge.

Preuss, H. (2007) The conceptualisation and measurement of mega sport event legacies. *Journal of Sport & Tourism* 12: 207–228.

Souliotis, N., Sayas, J., and Maloutas, T. (2014) Megaprojects, neoliberalization, and state capacities: Assessing the medium-term impact of the 2004 Olympic Games on Athenian urban policies. *Environment and Planning C: Government and Policy* 32: 731–745.

Tomlinson, A. (2014) Olympic legacies: Recurrent rhetoric and hard realities. *Contemporary Social Science* 9: 137–158.

Zimbalist, A. (ed.) (2017) *Rio 2016: Olympic Myths and Hard Realities.* Washington, DC: Brookings Institution Press.

Bibliography

Ainsworth-Wells, M. (2013) London's Olympic legacy: The results are in. *The Telegraph*.www.telegraph.co.uk/travel/destinations/europe/united-kingdom/england/london/articles/Londons-Olympic-legacy-the-results-are-in/

Atkin, R. (1980) Olympic voices for reform. *Christian Science Monitor*. www.csmonitor.com/1980/0212/021228.html

Atkinson, G., Mourato, S., Szymanski, S., and Ozdemiroglu, E. (2008) Are we willing to pay enough to back the bid?: Valuing the intangible impacts of London's bid to host the 2012 Summer Olympic Games. *Urban Studies* 45: 419–444.

Baade, R. A., Baumann, R., and Matheson, V. (2008) Slippery slope? Assessing the economic impact of the 2002 Winter Olympic Games in Salt Lake City. *Utah Economics Department Working Papers*. Paper 45. https://crossworks.holycross.edu/econ_working_papers/45

Baade, R. A. and Matheson, V. A. (2016). Going for the gold: The economics of the Olympics. *The Journal of Economic Perspectives* 30: 201–218.

Beans, L. (2014) 4 reasons the Sochi Olympics are an environmental disaster. *Ecowatch*. www.ecowatch.com/4-reasons-the-sochi-olympics-are-an-environmental-disaster-1881859802.html

Billings, S. B. and Holladay, J. S. (2012) Should cities go for the gold? The long-term impacts of hosting the Olympics. *Economic Inquiry* 50(3): 754–772.

Boykoff, J. (2016) *Power Games: A Political History of The Olympics*. London and New York: Verso.

Boyle, P. and Haggerty, K. D. (2009) Spectacular security: Mega-events and the sector complex. *International Political Sociology* 3: 257–274.

Brunet, F. (2005). *The Economic Impact of the Barcelona Olympic Games, 1986–2004: Barcelona: The Legacy of the Games, 1992–2002*. Barcelona: Centre d'Estudis Olímpics UAB. http://olympicstudies.uab.es/pdf/wp084_eng.pdf

Calvert, J. (2002) How to buy the Olympics. *Observer Sport Monthly* 21: 32–37.

Centre on Housing Rights and Evictions (2007) *Fair Play for Housing Rights: Mega-Events, Olympic Games and Housing Rights*. Geneva: Centre on Housing Rights and Evictions. www.ruig-gian.org/ressources/Report%20Fair%20Play%20FINAL%20FINAL%2020070531.pdf

Center on Housing Rights and Evictions (2008) *One World, Whose Dream? Housing Rights, Violations and the Beijing Games*. Geneva: Centre on Housing Rights and Evictions.

Dansero, E. and Mela, A. (2012) Bringing the mountains into the city: Legacy of the Winter Olympics, Turin 2006. In *The Palgrave Handbook of Olympic Studies* (pp. 178–194). UK: Palgrave Macmillan.

Debord, G. (1967) *The Society of the Spectacle*. New York: Zone Books.

Dyer, G. (2009) Beijing Olympics fails to boost tourism, figures show. *The Financial Times*.www.ft.com/content/6a0fd5ae-dd77-11dd-930e-000077b07658

Essex, S. and De Groot, J. (2016) The Winter Olympics; Driving urban change, 1924–2022. In Gold, J. and Gold, M. (eds.), *Olympic Cities: City Agendas, Planning and the World's Games, 1896–2020* (pp. 64–89). London: Routledge.

Feddersen, A. and Maennig, W. (2013) Employment effects of the Olympic Games in Atlanta 1996 reconsidered. *International Journal of Sport Finance* 8: 95–111.

Filipov, D. (2017) Sochi: A $50 billion dream come true? *The Washington Post*, November 16: p. A12.

Flyvberg, B. and Stewart, A. (2012) Olympic proportions: Cost and cost overrun and the Olympics 1960–2012. *Said Business School Working Paper*. University of Oxford. http://eureka.sbs.ox.ac.uk/4943/1/SSRN-id2382612_(2).pdf

Forrest, B. (2014) Putin's run for gold. *Vanity Fair*. www.vanityfair.com/news/politics/2014/02/sochi-olympics-russia-corruption

Fourie, J. and Santana-Gallego, M. (2011) The impact of mega-sport events on tourist arrivals. *Tourism Management* 32: 1364–1370.

Freeman, J. (2014) Raising the flag over Rio de Janeiro's favelas: Citizenship and social control in the Olympic city. *Journal of Latin American Geography* 13: 7–38.

Gibson, O. (2016) How West Ham struck the deal of the century with Olympic stadium move. *The Guardian*. www.theguardian.com/football/2016/apr/14/west-ham-deal-century-olympic-stadium

Giesecke, J. A. and Madden, J. R. (2011) Modelling the economic impacts of the Sydney Olympics in retrospect – Game over for the bonanza story? *Economic Papers: A Journal of Applied Economics and Policy* 30(2): 218–232. doi:10.1111/j.1759-3441.2011.00109.x

Goldblatt, D. (2016) *The Games: A Global History of the Olympics*. New York: W. W. Norton.

Gratton, C. and Preuss, H. (2008) Maximizing Olympic impacts by building up legacies. *The International Journal of the History of Sport* 25: 1922–1938.

The Guardian (2017) Rio Olympics venues already falling into a state of disrepair. www.theguardian.com/sport/2017/feb/10/rio-olympic-venues-already-falling-into-a-state-of-disrepair

Guttman, A. (2002, 2nd ed.) *The Olympics: A History of the Modern Games*. Urbana and Chicago: University of Illinois Press.

Hotchkiss, J. L., Moore, R. E., and Rios-Avila, F. (2015). Reevaluation of the employment impact of the 1996 Summer Olympic Games. *Southern Economic Journal* 81: 619–632.

Hotchkiss, J. L., Moore, R. E., and Zobay, S. M. (2003) Impact of the 1996 Summer Olympic Games on employment and wages in Georgia. *Southern Economic Journal*, 691–704.

IOC (2014) *Olympic Agenda 2020: 20 + 20 Recommendations.* https://stillmed. olympic.org/Documents/Olympic_Agenda_2020/Olympic_Agenda_2020-20-20_Recommendations-ENG.pdf

IOC (International Olympic Committee) (2007) *The Top Program.* Geneva: IOC.

Jasmand, S. and Maennig, W. (2008) Regional income and employment effects of the 1972 Munich Summer Olympic Games. *Regional Studies* 42: 991–1002.

Jonas, A. E. and Wilson, D. (1999) *The Urban Growth Machine: Critical Perspectives, Two Decades Later.* Albany: SUNY Press.

Kasimati, E. (2003) Economic aspects and the Summer Olympics: A review of related research. *International Journal of Tourism Research* 5: 433–444.

Kassens-Noor, E. (2012) *Planning Olympic Legacies: Transport Dreams and Urban Realities.* London and New York: Routledge.

Kassens-Noor, E. (2013) Transport legacy of the Olympic Games 1992–2012. *Journal of Urban Affairs* 35: 393–416.

Kassens-Noor, E. (2015) The legacy of the 2004 Olympic for the Athens transport system. In *Routledge Handbook of Sport and Legacy: Meeting the Challenge of Major Sports Events* (pp. 131–141). London: Routledge.

Kennelly, J. (2017) Symbolic violence and the Olympic Games: Low-income youth, social legacy commitments, and urban exclusion in Olympic host cities. *Journal of Youth Studies* 20: 145–161.

Kennelly, J., and Watt, P. (2011) Sanitizing public space in Olympic host cities: The spatial experiences of marginalized youth in 2010 Vancouver and 2012 London. *Sociology* 45: 765–781.

Kim, J., Kang, J. H., and Kim, Y.-K. (2014) Impact of mega sport events on destination image and country image. *Sport Marketing Quarterly* 23: 161–175.

Kirkup, N. and Major, B. (2006) Doctoral foundation paper: The reliability of economic impact studies of the Olympic Games: A post-games study of Sydney 2000 and considerations for London 2012. *Journal of Sport & Tourism* 11: 275–296.

Klauser, F. R. (2015) Interacting forms of expertise and authority in mega-event security: The example of the 2010 Vancouver Olympic Games. *Geographical Journal* 181: 224–234.

Liu, D. and Wilson, R. (2014) The negative impacts of hosting mega-sporting events and intention to travel: A test of the crowding-out effect using the London 2012 Games as an example. *International Journal of Sports Marketing and Sponsorship* 15: 12–26.

Longman, J. (2000) Olympic: Leaders of Salt Lake City Olympic bid are indicted in bribery scandal. *The New York Times.*www.nytimes.com/2000/07/21/sports/olympics-leaders-of-salt-lake-olympic-bid-are-indicted-in-bribery-scandal.html

Maennig, W. and Richter, F. (2012). Exports and Olympic Games: Is there signal a effect? *Journal of Sports Economics* 13(6): 635–641.

McDonald, R. (1980) Greece could become permanent site for Olympics. *The Chicago Tribune.*http://archives.chicagotribune.com/1980/03/09/page/53/article/greece-could-become-permanent-site-of-olympics

Molotch, H. (1976) The city as a growth machine: Toward a political economy of place. *American Journal of Sociology* 82: 309–332.

Muller, M. (2014) After Sochi: Costs and benefits of Russia's Olympic Games. *Eurasian Geography and Economics* 55: 628–655.

Müller, M. (2015) The mega-event syndrome: Why so much goes wrong in mega-event planning and what to do about it. *Journal of the American Planning Association* 81: 6–17.

Müller, M. (2016) How megaevents capture their hosts: Event seizure and The World Cup 2018 in Russia. *Urban Geography* 1–20.

Olivier, R. and Lauermann, J. (2017) *Failed Olympic Bids and the Transformation of Urban Space*. London: Palgrave.

Orttung, R. W. and Zhemukhov, S. (2014) The 2014 Sochi Olympic mega-project and Russia's political economy. *East European Politics* 30: 175–191.

Perottet, T. (2004) *The Naked Olympics: The True Story of the Ancient Games*. New York: Random.

Porter, P. K. and Fletcher, D. (2008) The economic impact of the Olympic Games: Ex ante predictions and ex poste reality. *Journal of Sport Management* 22: 470–486.

Preuss, H. (2004). *The Economics of Staging The Olympics: A Comparison of the Games, 1972–2008*. Cheltenham: Edward Elgar Publishing.

Renson, R. and den Hollander, M. (1997) Sport and business in the city: The Antwerp Olympic Games of 1920 and the urban elite. *Olympika* VI: 73–84.

Rose, A. K. and Spiegel, M. M. (2011) The Olympic effect. *Economic Journal* 121: 652–677.

Shin, H. B. and Bingqin L. (2013) Whose games? The costs of being "Olympic citizens" in Beijing. *Environment and Urbanization*. http://eprints.lse.ac.uk/52676/1/Shin_Whose_games_costs_2013.pdf

Short, J. R. (2008) Globalization, cities and the Summer Olympics. *City* 12: 321–340.

Short, J. R. (2015) We should host the Olympics in the same place everytime. *The Washington Post*.www.washingtonpost.com/posteverything/wp/2015/07/28/we-should-host-the-olympics-in-the-same-place-every-time/

Siddons, L. (1999) IOC expels six members in Salt Lake City scandal. *The Guardian*. www.theguardian.com/sport/1999/mar/17/ioc-expels-members-bribes-scandal

Swaddling, J. (2015, 3rd ed.) *The Ancient Olympic Games*. London: British Museum Press and University of Texas Press.Tien, C., Lo, H. C., and Lin, H. W. (2011) The economic benefits of mega events: A myth or a reality? A longitudinal study on the Olympic Games. *Journal of Sport Management* 25: 11–23.

Tomlinson, A. (2014) Olympic legacies: Recurrent rhetoric and hard realities. *Contemporary Social Science* 9: 137–158.

Toohey, K. and Taylor, T. (2012) Surveillance and securitization: A forgotten Sydney Olympic legacy. *International Review for the Sociology of Sport* 47: 324–337.

Vasilyeva, N. (2015) Oligarchs unload Sochi Olympic assets to recoup investment. *The Morning Call*. www.mcall.com/sports/olympics/mc-olympics-russia-sochi-costly-legacy-20150207-story.html#page=1

Von Rekowsky, R. (2013) Are the Olympics a gold opportunity for investors? *Fideilty Investments: Investment Insights*. www.fidelity.com/bin-public/060_www_fidelity_com/documents/Are%20the%20Olympics%20a%20Golden%20Opportunity%20for%20Investors_Fidelity.pdf

Wagg, S. (2015) *The London Olympics of 2012: Politics, Promises and Legacy.* London: Palgrave Macmillan.

Wilson, S. (2016) The Olympics are having an unprecedented meltdown. *Business Insider*.www.businessinsider.com/the-olympics-are-having-an-unprecedented-meltdown-2016-5

Woff, R. (1999) *The Ancient Greek Olympics*. New York: Oxford University Press.

Yamawaki, Y. and Duarte, F. (2014) Olympics and legacy in Sydney: Urban transformation and real estate a decade after the Games. *Journal of Urban Design* 19: 511–540.

Zimbalist, A. (2016, 2nd ed.) *Circus Maximus: The Economic Gamble Behind Hosting the Olympics and World Cup.* Washington, DC: Brookings Institution Press.

Zimbalist, A. (ed.) (2017) *Rio 2016: Olympic Myths and Hard Realities.* Washington, DC: Brookings Institution Press.

Index